I0559591

Almost Unloved

By

Elizabeth Stewart

Copyright © 2024

Elizabeth Stewart

Paperback ISBN: 979-8-9891928-5-4

Hardcover ISBN: 979-8-9891928-4-7

Published by:

LT-Writing

All Rights Reserved. Any unauthorized reprinting or use of this material is strictly prohibited. No part of this book may be reproduced or transmitted in any form or by any means, electronic or mechanical, including photocopying, recording, or by any information storage and retrieval system without express written permission from the author.

TABLE OF CONTENTS

Part 1: Roots

Chapter 1: The Making of Mary

On a bitter Chicago winter morning in 1956, Mary and her two children weave through the relentless swarms of people at the train station. She struggles with bulky bags in one hand and little Kathy on her hip. Train whistles blow over bustling conversations and the bellowing of porters carrying piles of bags up and down the platform.

A porter hurries up to Mary and asks, "Can I help you with your bags, ma'am?"

She stops for just a second and smiles politely. Her sparkling green eyes glanced up at him. "No, thank you, sir. We're fine."

She continues as if on a mission; the porter watches the beautiful dark-haired woman with shapely legs disappear into the crowd.

They board the *El Capitan* in the evening for the 13-hour trip to San Diego. It was there that Mary would find refuge in her latest predicament. After shuffling to their seats, Mary removes an old blanket and four small, well-worn toys before stuffing their belongings into the overhead compartment. She removes her favorite fur-lined brown coat and a colorful scarf and covers her two small children.

Taking her seat, she sighs as she loosens her clothing. She smiles at her children playing quietly with their toys and then looks out of the gritty train window caked with smog residue. The grey muck reminds her of her various betrayals and secrets. Her smile is now a determination to escape the demons that tried to destroy her essence. The train pulls out, and the tracks play a melodious tapping that lulls her into a feeling of false security. Completely exhausted, Mary closes her eyes, holding back tears as she often does. Her emotional defense mechanisms have broken down just enough to feel something. Her entire life, she's tried to learn how to live by the strict Christian rules that her family insisted upon while still bearing her childhood's emotional and physical scars.

Her father, Cyril, a robust Baptist deacon and carpenter by trade, was a solemn, hard-working man, showing his children little love and patience.

Without her father's guidance and emotional presence, Mary never learned how a man should cherish and love her. Cyril was much better at doling out punishments. He was "The Law," and his children would not be disobedient heathens and bring shame into his house. When boundaries were tested, the children often felt the stinging welts that came from the blows of his thick razor strap. The rod of correction wasn't spared. To make matters worse, the motherly love to soothe those wounds was also absent.

Mary's mother, Myrtle, was a stout woman who sometimes could be hostile towards her children. It was as if she resented having children; that lack of a good example left her feeling inadequate. Myrtle's mother, Mary Ellen, died at thirty-three from the swine flu pandemic in 1918, leaving eight children with an absent, dispassionate, and unavailable father to fend for themselves in an age of poverty, disease, and hunger. Things got so desperate that John William, Myrtle's father, had to send five of his middle children to the Mother's Jewel's orphanage in York, Nebraska, for fear that they would starve. Myrtle had a keen sense of survival but lacked maternal instinct. Her insensitive heart and looming depression overcame her children like an infection engulfing them as time passed.

Myrtle worked diligently in the church and, by all appearances, was a good-natured, obedient preacher's wife. But Mary knew the dark side of her mother hidden behind closed doors. There was this unspoken swear of secrecy in the family. Giving the illusion of a happy, God-fearing household was rule number one.

Mary was the firstborn of five and thus responsible for her siblings. She became Myrtle's scapegoat anytime something went wrong. Several times, without justification, she bore the burden when the other children would not follow the rules. Mary's confusion and hurt feelings welled inside her like sludge, ready to ooze out in anger, resentment, and rebelliousness.

By age fourteen, Mary's unyielding longing for affection sent her fleeing in search of love and attention in all the wrong places. She had a determined spirit; like any human being, she wanted validation that she was worth loving. She found older guys more understanding; however, they had sexual needs that Mary was not emotionally ready to handle. It wasn't long until she found a young man willing to take advantage of her need for affection and validation. She deeply understood her worth and love when she was with him. He was like a drug that numbed her tragic life for a time, and she craved that escape increasingly.

Hiding the relationship proved challenging as she became careless with whoever saw her. Neighbors began to talk about the "unruly deacon's daughter," which prompted her parents to send her to a house for wayward girls. Mary's heart only hardened against her parents, further breeding bitterness and anger. Incidentally, the only lesson Mary learned in the six months she was away was how to hone her skills at hiding her rebelliousness. Her parents had no clue how to deal with such a "promiscuous" and "defiant" girl, as even the "rod of correction" could not beat her into submission.

She became bolder as time passed, returning home after a date with a guy she'd been seeing. He reached over to kiss her goodnight before she went inside. Mary's mother glared in a seething rage behind the curtain before storming through the door onto the porch, screaming, "You little tramp! You get in this house right now!" Mary felt humiliated and clenched her fists as she swiftly walked through the door. She could feel her face flush; she was about to scream aloud with boiling anger that would shake the windows.

Myrtle was already in a fury like the devil had occupied her residence. In a moment of rage, without thought of consequence, she picked up a wooden chair and broke it on Mary's back. The swift blow left Mary in groaning pain, crumpled on the floor in the fetal position. Before barreling out of the room, her mother said. "Your father will hear nothing of this; you've put him through enough pain," slamming the door behind her. Picking her weary bones from the wood floor, Mary rushed toward her bed and lay there with stinging tears streaming down her face. They were not remorse but tears of resentment for being born to a family that couldn't love her. She swallowed tears that now set like concrete deep within Mary's heart. Just one more layer to the wall she must build around her heart for survival. As the bruises developed across her back, desperate plans to leave home plagued her thoughts.

At just sixteen, Mary met Robert. He was handsome with dark, well-groomed hair and penetrating blue eyes. At eighteen, Robert was strong, charismatic, and independent. Mary was instantly captivated, and he spent every moment turning up the charm, making himself look like her hero. After a brief courtship, she was pregnant with their first child, and they married. However, Mary soon learned that her self-indulgent mother-in-law, Janice, played Robert like a puppet. Her influence was the inner 'strength' he displayed if Mary didn't like something. Janice would not let a little tramp take her rightful place on the throne of control, so she had to break Mary down. She constantly degraded Mary to Robert, speaking little jabs here and there until, eventually, Robert started to complain about the same things. Janice dictated all aspects of their lives. She always commented on how their house should look and what they should eat. She impressed Mary with dressing and acting to "please her husband." Over time, the emotional abuse Mary endured turned physical when she would get out of line or try to challenge things.

 Even when the family needed money, Robert wouldn't allow his wife to get a job for fear that she would find another hero and he would lose control of her. He joined the Military to support the family. Mary was excited initially, but to her dismay, his fondness for alcohol and lousy temper ended in a dishonorable discharge. Add to that his lack of self-esteem, and you have a recipe for disaster. As his drinking worsened, Mary felt hopeless to learn she was pregnant again. By some miracle, she persuaded him to get help in the sanitarium. After his discharge, it wasn't long until he returned to his old vices: the bottle and his fist.

After another brutal attack on Mary, Robert was arrested and forced back into the sanitarium. She would not let him get another chance to use her as a punching bag. Before his release, she arranged to stay with her parents and threatened divorce if he touched her again. Mary secured a job at a local diner, getting generous tips, and began to have a little self-confidence again. Robert kept coming around with that smile and slick talk. As tension mounted at her parents' house, she thought about Kenny growing up without his father and slipping into his soft words. He convinced her he had changed as apologies slipped carelessly from his mouth. She wanted to believe him. She needed him to be the hero she imagined when they first met, and she finally gave in. For a few months, things were going great. He was a doting husband and father, and Mary wanted to be happy, though she struggled to trust him. By the birth of their second child, Kathy, Mary had again succumbed to living within the parameters of her mother-in-law's control through Robert. The bittersweet announcement of her daughter only solidified her fears that she would never be free of Robert and his abuse.

Though Mary welcomed the quiet times he was in the drunk tank, he always returned to torment her. She dared not leave because her mother-in-law forced her loyalty, using her grandchildren as leverage. The words haunted her. *"If you even think about leaving my son and taking those kids, I promise you will never see them again."* Janice's threats terrified Mary. Her children represented the only good in her life. Where could she run? As Robert got weaker in the chokehold of the bottle, he gradually loosened control of his wife. Not even his overbearing mother could control what alcohol had turned into a rag doll. It was up to Mary to support the family. He was in no condition. Mary had the perfect opportunity to surmise a careful escape two years in the making.

The chores she learned as a child served her well as she made clothes and started canning fruits and vegetables for extra cash. Mary continued her work as a server in downtown Chicago, and to make extra money, she briefly worked as a taxi driver, the first woman in Chicago to do that job.

She was excited at the prospect of meeting new people in an alternate world where she could be herself, whatever that was. Her children also gave her the emotional strength to forge ahead, never dwelling on her beginnings.

His incapacity surpassed Robert's inability to support his family to love his wife and children. It was time to leap. Mary knew if she stayed any longer, she would surely die, emotionally or physically, losing herself in the daily battle to survive. She finally had the fortitude to leave that life behind and make a new beginning. Her new home would be a little basement apartment below her parents' house.

Mary continued to work to support the family while her mother watched the children. She longed for the day she could move away from them, but where she was now was better than where she was.

In the summer of 1955, during her separation from Robert, Mary was working a long shift at the diner. She was cleaning a table when she glanced up at a tall, broad-shouldered stranger with wavy, sandy hair. He stood confidently in his faded jeans and boots as if he had just stepped out of a motorcycle magazine. "Hello, I'm Ken – Mary, right?" he asked, pointing at her name tag.

Mary caught her breath, "Yes. What can I do for you?"

As their eyes met, she felt something she hadn't felt in a very long time... a longing passion for wanting to be somewhere else, anywhere else, with him. But then, Ken revealed that he was married, convinced her the marriage wasn't working out, and that Mary made him feel alive again. Technically, she was still married, so she was more than understanding of his situation. She felt a connection with him that she couldn't share with another.

Over the next four months, they spent every free minute together. Ken was her solace and an escape from an unfulfilled life. Was this finally her chance at living and loving? Could this beautiful Mary bloom amongst the weeds of her past?

Autumn leaves are starting to change into their vibrant colors with the new season, and Mary finds herself changing, too. The couple's hot July romance has yielded an unexpected package. It has been seven weeks since her last period, and Mary is pregnant with Ken's baby. She is eager but scared to share her news with the man she knows will be a great daddy. Finally, her children will grow up knowing how a man is supposed to raise a family. She reasoned that this child was a message from God, that this would be her escape from brutality.

Later that day, Ken stepped into the café as he had done many times before, carrying his helmet. After all these months, Mary still felt goosebumps on her skin and warmth in her heart.

She took him aside, hugged him, and whispered, "I have exciting news. I will burst if I don't tell you immediately!"

He looked at her confused with a slight smile and patiently waited for her to continue. Mary squealed, "I'm going to have our baby."

He pulled her away abruptly, "What! How could you let this happen? How could you get pregnant? What are you thinking?"

Mary panicked. *This was not her Ken. Why would he act like this? Why would he say these words?*

"I...I thought you loved me." Mary stuttered.

Ken grabbed her shoulders and made her look at him in his angry eyes, "Loved you?? Mary, I'm married. We were having fun. I thought you understood that. You're great, but...ahhhh... this is not what I wanted. This is...too complicated." Ken turned around to walk out the door, but Mary ran after him and stood before him.

"Wait! What am I going to do? You led me to believe that you loved me!" Her eyes begged him to reconsider as they welled up with tears.

"Mary, you foolish girl! Did you think I wanted to raise another guy's kids?" His frustration mounted. "Look, you need to take care of it. Take this money and do what you have to, but leave me out of it, and don't bother me with this again." He shoved a wad of bills into her trembling hand and was gone with that.

Mary watched speechless through the glass door as he rode away on his motorcycle. She felt numb, oblivious to her customers' condescending stares. Tears fell to the floor as she turned toward the storage room.

Her demeanor quickly changed from desperation to frustration at herself. What *did you expect, Mary? Isn't this the way your life is? Did you think happiness was possible for you?*

At twenty, Mary lived a lifetime of disappointment. She had two children, one on the way, and she was still married to a man who loved the bottle more than he would ever love her. Her heart didn't want to believe she was destined for loneliness and abuse. Her mind tried to rationalize. *No, he's simply scared. I must try again after he has had time to think about it.*

Mary let a week pass before standing at the door of a small brick house in Arlington Heights, on the outskirts of Chicago. She didn't know what she would say to him, but she had to understand what had happened. She knocked, and his wife, visibly round with child, answered the door. Mary wasn't surprised to see another woman standing there after Ken had told her.

"Is Ken home?" Mary asked.

His wife answered, "I'm sorry, he's not here now. What do you need?"

Mary stuttered as she said, "I know Ken from the diner. He comes in and sees me all the time. I need to talk with him about something personal."

She looked at Mary. "I told you he's not here, and I don't take kindly to other women talking with him in private, so don't come back."

The woman closed the heavy wooden door in her face. Sobbing, she turned and walked away. She wandered the streets of Chicago for hours, bewildered. *How could he turn his back on me after telling me how much he loved me? What kind of a man cheats on his pregnant wife?*

Days faded into weeks; Mary fell into a deep depression as her situation grew more hopeless every minute. It wasn't comfortable living in the tiny space below her parents. Still, she became an expert at hiding her distended belly under her girdle and loose clothes over the next few months.

Seeing a doctor would raise too many questions, and she desperately needed to hide what her parents would surely dub her bastard child. She feared they would take away both her children for this indiscretion. She needed to talk to someone, but the last time she ran to her father for words of wisdom, he only said, "You made your bed; now lie in it!" Where would she go from here? Mary thought about abortion for about two minutes, then decided this was not an option

The fifties were desperate times for unwed mothers, and Mary knew about the horror stories of self-abortions with coat hangers and knitting needles. Women, too scared to face society's expectations or their parents, risked their lives to eliminate their illegitimate babies. Abortion was an illegal procedure done by butchers in alleyways. Several "doctors" operated out of sympathy for the girls. Still, many non-medical people did it to make a quick buck at the cost of countless women's lives. Mary knew the consequences of a botched-up procedure. Even if she survived the process, she might never be able to carry another child. Aside from that, her belief in God wouldn't allow her to take that step. What are the alternatives? She could move to the other side of Chicago and vanish with the kids, but there wasn't enough money for the family, even with two jobs. For now, she would play the waiting game and pray an answer would come to her soon.

On Christmas Day, almost five months into the pregnancy, her prayers were answered when she saw a greeting card her mother received from her sister Grace. She opened the card and saw her aunt's number and a new address. Mary's heart leaped as she thought through the possibilities.

It was well known that Myrtle did not like Grace and was very jealous of Grace's close relationship with their Father. Grace laughed at Myrtle's misfortunes as a teenager because Myrtle was the family tattletale who always caused the other children to be beaten by their father with the strap. Given the strained relationship between her mother and Grace, Mary was sure her secret would be safe with Grace.

Hurrying home from work one day, Mary stops at a pay phone and calls Grace Collect in San Diego, CA.

"Hello." A raspy voice on the other side of the phone answered.

"Hello, Aunt Grace. Is that you?" Mary said.

"Yes, who is this?"

"It's Mary, Myrtle's oldest daughter. Do you remember meeting me at Grandfather's funeral?"

"Yes, how are you doing? Is everything all right?" Grace inquired.

Mary hesitated, thinking back to the funeral. *"If you ever need a place to stay away from your overbearing, self-indulgent mother, you can always come live with us."* Had Aunt Grace meant it, or was it an attempt to jab back at her sister? Either way, Mary was running out of options.

"Oh yes, everyone is fine. I was wondering … what I mean is… do you remember telling me if I ever needed a place to stay or had a problem, that all I had to do was ask?"

"Yes, of course, what's wrong?"

Mary tears up and continues, "Aunt Grace, I am in serious trouble here. Did you mean what you said at grandfather's funeral?"

"Of course I did."

Mary hesitated, cleared her throat, and said, "If it's not too much to ask, I need to take you up on that offer."

Sensing the urgency in her voice, Grace inquired, "When? What's wrong? Are you ok?"

"No, I'm so confused I don't know what to do. I've gone over this repeatedly, and all I can think about is I have to get out of Chicago for a couple of months."

Grace asked again, "What's wrong, Mary? You're not making any sense. Are you in trouble with the law?"

Mary said in a quivering voice, "No, it's nothing like that, but…I messed up Aunt Grace. I need someone to rely on right now. I promise I will explain everything after I get there."

There was a brief silence at the other end. Mary slowly raised her head and gazed up as if she were waiting for a sign from God. In her despair, she only noticed the graffiti on the top of the phone booth. **"There is light even for those who are blind."** She doubted *those* words would help her now.

"Do you need any money to come to San Diego?" inquired Grace.

"I have enough for the kids and me to get train tickets. I need time and distance to figure out what to do."

"Come see me, Mary. We will figure it out together."

"Oh, thank you so much. I appreciate this. I'll call you soon with the details of my arrival."

"Okay, Mary. Bye."

A glimmer of hope rose within Mary as she hung up the phone.

Mary hurried to the train station after work the next day, hoping Janice wouldn't suspect anything unusual.

She called Grace Collect the following day to tell her when she would arrive.

"Hi, Aunt Grace. I'm calling to confirm that I bought the tickets yesterday."

Grace was excited, "Great! How are all the loose ends coming along?"

"I still have to quit my job and find an excuse to leave here with both kids."

"That's easy! Just tell them you need a vacation. Besides, you can work here as well as there. I can't wait for you to get here! There is so much to do and see in San Diego! We'll have so much fun getting to know one another."

Mary was still trying to figure out what to do about her growing belly and wasn't sharing in the excitement, but she tried to be positive anyway.

"I will talk with my parents this evening about the trip. I'll think of something to say. Thanks again, Grace; I'll see you in about two weeks."

Lying to her family was a nightmare she thought she would never survive. Still, she managed to convince them she needed to get away to think about the fate of her marriage.

Mary jolted as someone bumped into her seat while going down the tiny passageway of the train. She looks down at her sleeping children beside her and rubs her swollen belly. *How can I live? What will I do if I lose my babies? I know they will take my kids if they find out.*

Mary can't bear the thought that her actions might one day bring shame to her in their eyes. Her children depend on her, but more than that, they still look up to her.

She spies a clock along the wall in the passageway. She hadn't dozed long. Los Angeles was still 10 hours away. No matter what happens next…she has time, distance, and an ally in Grace.

Chapter 2: Indecisive Choices

The train pulls into the station early the following day. Mary tugs at her colorful mid-length skirt. She gathers her children and steps out of the compartment they have called home for thirteen hours.

The warm California weather was a welcome contrast to Chicago. The soft, salty breeze caressed Mary's face as she took in the ocean air. Scantily dressed people rushed off to their destinations. The morning sun created a landscape of glowing oranges and yellows filtered by fluffy clouds across a soft blue sky.

As she looks around, she sees Grace at the end of the ramp. Mary watches the stocky woman with long, dark, straight hair approach. She wears bright red lipstick and has penciled in her eyebrows.

The sight makes Mary smile, but she cannot get past the feeling that she is "just here on business." They exchanged hellos, gathered the kids, and picked up the bags.

"You look tired, Mary. Didn't you get any sleep on the train?"

Mary sighed, "Honestly, every time I closed my eyes, I thought about what brought me here and the decisions I had to make."

Mary is exceptionally swollen today from travel, and Grace cannot help but notice the bump under her skirt. Seeing Grace was eyeing the belly and the unborn child, Mary explained her situation, starting with what had transpired since her separation from Robert last spring.

Mary paused. "Grace, they'll take my kids if they find out about this baby." She started to sob, "I can't lose my kids. How could I be so naive?"

Trying to console her, Grace said, "Everything will be fine. Let's think this through."

Grace pondered for a second. *This could be a perfect opportunity for her.* "Have you decided what to do about the baby yet?" she asked.

Mary could hardly fathom the solution, "I'm not sure at this point; I might have to give the baby up. I've thought hard about that and may have no other choice."

With the luggage and the kids packed in, they start on their way in the dusty old 1954 maroon Packard with brown velvet seats. There was a distinct smell of Bob's Sir Walter Raleigh pipe tobacco in the car.

Mary gazes at the palm trees lining the neighborhood streets as they slip into the morning traffic on the three-hour drive to San Diego. The hum of the car has a relaxing sound; even the kids are still, giving the impression that California, too, is calm.

Grace interrupts the silence. "How could you get yourself into such a mess? Was your life so desperate you didn't care he was married?"

Holding back the tears, Mary scrambled for the words to explain that she hadn't even been able to explain to herself.

"I never thought my life would come to this. I'm overcome with so many emotions I don't know which one to feel first. Sometimes, it's easier to let the numbness take over so I can have some peace, but it never really makes anything better."

Grace glances over as Mary continues.

"I thought he loved me, you know. I honestly thought he was the one who was going to stand by me. I just wanted to be happy for once in my life."

Grace snickered, "Ha! You ought to know better than to think any man could improve your life. Nobody cares about your happiness."

Mary couldn't help but hear her own mother's voice of hurt and betrayal in Grace's comment. What could have happened to them that would have caused such bitterness? The empathetic friendship was enough to stir up anger.

"I am so mad that he thought he could use me! What kind of creep looks you in your eyes and tells you he wants to be with you and your kids while cheating on his pregnant wife?"

Grace softened and began to tell her story. A hardened heart resulted from two prior failed marriages: one to a severely abusive and controlling husband who kept her in their apartment by taping the door, and if the tape tore, he beat her. The other was a rambling baseball player who cheated. What did she know about stability or love? Now, she was married to a Navy sailor who was never home,  which was OK with Grace because she could spend time with her friends and other men. The cynicism within Grace was epic, but at least Grace knew what it was like to be deceived by a man, which brought comfort. Mary still couldn't shake the feeling that she was on shaky ground in this new place.

Grace was known to be one of the most pessimistic people you would ever meet. Even if the sky were clear and bright, Grace would find a way to make the storm clouds appear.

She was a self-serving, manipulative woman who managed to find a way to be helpful to others when it suited her.

She wasn't as physically abusive as Myrtle, but their upbringing made her just as emotionally vacant. The idea of having a new baby consumed Grace. She knew if she got what she wanted, she would have to try to console Mary.

The car turns into the driveway at 1002 19th Street, past all the other little white wooden houses, at the opening of a white picket fence. Their yard is a decent size, although mostly dirt. The house extends across the front but is not very deep, about the size of a double-wide trailer. On the right side of the house, a white wood-frame garage was converted into a tool shed for all of Bob's used auto parts.

An old white wooden door stands in the exact middle of the long house. Through the front screen door, you can see the cozy little kitchen. The walls are a dingy mustard color with peeling paint. The sticky film on the walls and the smell of old tar and nicotine reveal Grace's nasty habit.

Mary smiles politely and asks, "What room would you like us to stay in?"

"You can all stay in the back bedroom. I borrowed a small bed from the landlord to sleep on while you're here. The full-sized bed back there wouldn't be enough room for all of you."

Mary glances into the hallway from the kitchen. The hallway has a door on each side leading to the bedrooms.

"It's the door to the left in the hallway," said Grace.

Mary looks at Grace with grateful eyes, "Thank you...for helping me out." Then, she leads the kids into the room and lays them down to sleep.

Mary feels a bittersweet liberation from the relentless reigns of oppression that plagued her. Although temporary, Janice, her husband, and her meddling mother could no longer make her life miserable.

Looking down at her children, *I want them to know a better life. God helped me make the choices I needed to make to provide a better life for us all.* She knew God must be out there... somewhere. Otherwise, she would not have survived the hell she's been through.

She walks to the living room and sees Grace bringing bags from the car. Grace knows her sister Myrtle is mean and spiteful, and a small part of her feels sorry for her niece.

"You know it's always been lonely here with Bob out to sea."

"What does he look like? Do you have any pictures?"

Grace goes to the drawer to get the pictures. "He has broad shoulders. He reminds me of John Wayne because he's slightly bow-legged. Oh, and he walks with a slight limp. A mine exploded, and pieces exploded into his upper leg in WWII." She hands Mary the pictures.

"He's got thick black hair. And look at those big brown eyes!" Mary asked, "Does he have family here as well?"

"No, his mother died in childbirth. He was her only child. His father raised him in Mannington, West Virginia. Bob worked in the coal mines from the time he was fourteen. He came up for the draft when war broke out, so at seventeen, he decided to go into the Navy." Grace smiled.

"How long will he be gone this time?"

"Oh, he won't be back for at least three months. The Navy usually keeps him out for eight months or more."

Mary's expression changes, "What will I do about the baby? How can I adopt the baby without anyone finding out?" Sobbing, she says, "How can I ever come to terms with giving up my child?"

Grace puts her arm around her niece, "Would you consider letting Bob and me raise the child? I had a hysterectomy and can't have children, so this would be a welcome addition to my home."

Mary wondered why her aunt couldn't have children. "If you don't mind me asking, you've never explained what happened, Grace. Why can't you have children?"

Grace turns around. She hates telling the story because it brings back so much emotional trauma.

"I normally tell people who ask that I fell skating."

"So, you didn't lose the baby during a skating accident?"

"Ha, I've never been on skates, Mary."

Grace sighed, "It wasn't an accident. My second husband, Bud, and I weren't ready for children. He told me to get rid of it. So, I did. I went to a doctor who was doing abortions by the harbor. If I knew I couldn't have any more babies because of that butcher, I would have never agreed to the procedure."

Mary's stomach churned as Grace explained the pain and shame of allowing someone to take her baby away. She winces as she describes the searing pain that surged when the doctor inserted the instrument through her cervix and ripped the tiny fetus out of her body.

"He perforated my uterus, resulting in internal bleeding. I thought the bleeding and pain were normal until I could no longer ignore it. I had such a bad infection the Doctors did a hysterectomy to save my life."

Grace tears, "So you can understand why I would love to have a child to fill this void in my life."

"How do you think Uncle Bob will feel about all this?"

"I can write him to find out how he feels." Grace said, "I'm sure he'll be happy about it. He loves our friend's babies."

"If we go through this, it must be private," Mary said. No one can ever know this child is mine."

"We could tell the Navy I had a child while Bob was out to sea."

"It sounds too easy, Grace. What about the birth certificate?"

"We will work it out; don't worry about it now. I'll take care of all the paperwork."

Mary feels uneasy, but what alternatives did she have? *Thank God I didn't go through with the abortion. Leaving the child here is the only way; I have no choice. I must return to Chicago to face a life I hate, but I certainly cannot return the illegitimate child.*

"This would be easier if my mother understood what I was going through, Aunt Grace. She would just tell me what a slut I am. I won't ever be good enough for her."

"Now, Mary, don't start blaming yourself. Your mom had a tough childhood. We both grew up in the orphanage, which was a harsh place."

"I remember mom mentioning it to me once. She doesn't like to talk about it. How did you all end up there? Why didn't Grandpa keep you together?" Mary asks.

Grace took a deep breath, "Well, our mom died during The Great Pandemic of 1918, leaving eight of us behind, including the baby, to support." Grace pulls out a picture to show Mary.

"That's me in the middle of father's legs. Your mother is to the right of me. Dad couldn't make ends meet for all of us. We weren't starving, but work was hard to find. It was a tough time for everyone. Back then, orphanages were built to house large families because

thousands of parents died from influenza, leaving behind children who needed food and shelter. Considering our desperate circumstances, our father felt giving up the five middle children was the only way for us to survive."

"Is that why Mom is so hard-hearted and unforgiving?"

"No doubt, Mary. The matrons believed working hard would produce a sense of duty and keep idle hands from being the devil's tools. When we didn't stay in line, we were disciplined and put in closets until we did as we were told. I overcame most of my experiences; I'm guessing your mother could never move on."

"How long did you stay in that awful place?"

"When Father felt we were independent enough to care for ourselves, he eventually allowed us to return home. We left one by one as we got older. By the time I could move home, it was 1929, and I had been there for nine years. Father had become a carpenter. Financially, times were booming. Movie houses and new apartment buildings were popping up everywhere in Chicago.

We were in the middle of prohibition, and Al Capone had become the crime czar. Machine gun fire was prevalent in the streets as rival gangsters tried to rub out their competition. Your dad's brother, Elbert Lusader, got shot in the neck while driving his streetcar down Main Street. No one was safe from the gang wars."

Mary nods. "I've heard various stories about life in Chicago during that time. Of course, by the time I was born in December 1935, the FBI had a sensible handle on crime, and those days were just a memory."

Grace continued, "Since we were all separated in the orphanage, we didn't grow up together and had no real sense of family. As we became adults, we left and did not attempt to stay in touch. It was easier that way."

Despite the unwarranted punishments, now that Mary knows more about her mom's past, she sees things more clearly. *That orphanage had taken its toll. A flower can't flourish in a dark place without water.*

Mary looks back at Grace, "I'm going to get unpacked so I can go out to look for a job first thing tomorrow."

Grace nods, "We'll have to work out a schedule because I work nights, and someone should be here with the kids. There's no reason to pay for a babysitter, but if we need one, Mrs. Moler, the landlord's wife, is a nice lady and loves kids."

Mary smiled, "Thank you. I'm tired and need to get a little sleep."

Mary heads to her room.

Grace says, "Try not to worry so much. Everything will be all right. See you in the morning. Good night, dear."

Is Grace right? Will everything be OK? Will the baby be better off with them? What will life be like in San Diego? She hardly knew anything about Bob and Grace and had many unanswered questions.

The bedclothes Mary puts on are comfortable and warm. She slips wearily into the soft makeshift bed. There is no arguing, dirty dishes, or defending her life now. She closes her eyes, takes a deep breath, and listens to her children's breathing. Not long before she is asleep, her dreams are plagued by the decisions she must make. Does she risk losing two children to save one?

Mary is up early the following day after a restless and weary night. The baby inside her has been restless and thrashed about as if it knew the turn of events. Her kids had a tough night as well.

Little Kathy was never really a morning person. It was hard to motivate her, and this morning was no different. Waking up in a new place didn't help. Hungry and irritated at her new surroundings, she rubs her little green eyes and pushes the tangled, dirty blond hair from her face in frustration, whining about being held. Kenny, on the other hand, is a sweet, easygoing child. The change doesn't seem to affect him; he is his usual Grown-up self. Mary is grateful to find enough food in the refrigerator to feed the kids breakfast before letting them play outside.

"Kenny, keep an eye on your sister." He looks back at his mom and runs out the door, "Yes, Mommy."

 After cleaning off the table, Mary gets herself a cup of coffee and sits at the kitchen's small dinette table. She notices the tar-colored walls and flaking paint as she glances at Grace, who is already enjoying her breakfast of coffee and cigarettes.

"Maybe you should take some time to relax a few days before you go out and get a job right away," says Grace. "You are pregnant, and all this stress cannot benefit the baby."

"Yes…you are right. I'll take a day or two to catch up on my rest, but I must get a job soon. Besides, I would go crazy if I had to sit here and think about everything all the time. I could get a job at one of those diners we passed on the way down the strip."

"Good idea. I know a great little place you can go to. I go there all the time, and I can talk to my friend who works there for you." said Grace.

"Thank you, Grace. You're a lifesaver."

During the week, Mary gets up at 4:30 every morning to prepare for work. It is peaceful this early, and she feels a little better about this mess she calls her life. Her convenient 6 to 2 shift gives her mommy time with the kids before she puts them down for the night.

After breakfast, Grace sends the kids outside for the day, leaving Kenny to look after his baby sister while Grace naps. At just five years old, he is the 'big protector. Kenny must grow up fast to take on responsibility.

Grace works nights as a cook at a nearby bar. It's her home away from home, even when Robert comes home. In Grace's eyes, there is no better job than one where she can drink on the clock.

Mary notices that her aunt has a hangover nearly every morning and wonders if she made the right decision to come. She wants to believe Grace will be a good mother to her child if given the opportunity. All Grace needs is a child to replace the alcohol and fill the loneliness in her life. Besides, what other choice did Mary have right now?

After a while, Grace shows her niece and the kids the sights in San Diego, and they end up at the beach. The four have begun to spend time together, and Mary feels more at ease with her. She watches Grace as she holds Kenny and Kathy's hands while walking on the pier.

"Aunt Grace, I've been thinking a lot about our talk about the baby, and- …"

"Yes. Have you decided?" Grace eagerly interrupts.

Mary begins again cautiously, "I think it would be a good idea to leave the baby here, considering my circumstances. I am still concerned and scared about all of this. I worry that I'm making a big mistake."

"Everything is going to be fine. Keeping the baby in the family is the best thing you can do. Bob will be happy." He never thought we would have any children of our own. You'll see. We'll take care of this baby like it was our own."

Mary can't shake her uneasiness, but they spend the next two months making hospital arrangements, shopping for necessities, and discussing baby names.

"Bob's hunting buddy is named Lee, so I thought that no matter what sex the baby is, we can give it that middle name," said Grace.

Mary's face brightens as she thinks about the flow of the name. "Yes, that will work nicely. Robert Lee or Elizabeth Lee it is." Mary smiles, keeping her doubts about the impending resolution and hopes of returning to the child one day.

On April 6th, shortly after five in the morning, Mary woke to her first labor pain. Not wanting to miss the day's wages, she gets up and heads to work.

It will be a while before any *actual* labor starts.

She had barely finished the morning breakfast rush when the pain from her contractions started. Mary runs into the lady's room. Leaning over the sink, she looks up at her red face, dripping with beads of sweat. *I must get to the hospital.* Mary heads to the back office to call her aunt. As she opens the door, her water breaks, spilling amniotic fluid on the tiled floor. She doubles over in pain, gritting her teeth. When the contraction passes, she grabs paper towels to clean the floor. Then, Mary reaches for the phone.

"Grace? Can you pick me up? I've gone into labor, and my water just broke; I need to get to the hospital immediately."

"I'll be right there."

Mary leans against the hallway wall. Customers, aware that she is clearly in labor, offer help. Mary politely declines. The pain is relentless, and Mary slides to the floor. *Hurry, Grace, Hurry!* Her mind filled with what-ifs. Mary knows that no matter what happens now or how much she wishes her life were different, she already loves this baby, and it breaks her heart knowing she must give it up.

By the time Grace arrives at the diner, Mary can hardly walk. With a heavy breath, she asks, "Where…are…the kids?"

"I left them with Mrs. Moler so I could go in with you. I've been thinking about what you said about not wanting to leave the baby, and I thought it might be good if you don't see the baby," Grace says, "Don't you think it would be easier that way?"

Her face flushed, and she was sweating. She can hardly make herself sit in the seat of the car. She wants to scream. Instead, Mary takes a deep breath. "Grace, what are you thinking? I must stay for a while anyway; I will see the baby. Don't worry; I know what I must do."

They arrive at the emergency entrance of San Diego County General Hospital. Grace drops Mary off at the curb. "I'll park the car and be right in."

Mary holds tight to the metal rail and pulls herself up the stairs to the wide glass doors, tugging at her sticky skirt. The pressure is immense; Mary's contractions are unyielding. Instead of feeling relieved that her pregnancy is nearing its end, Mary can't help but think how this means she is a step closer to a decision she doesn't know she can live with. Nurses rush Mary into delivery while Grace sits in the waiting room.

Mary pushes hard when on the delivery table, quickly giving birth to what she later calls "the easiest baby she ever delivered." At 10:37 a.m., she gives birth to an eight lb. 1 oz. Baby girl with bright green eyes and white peach fuzz on her round head. The doctor puts the baby up on her chest. She is healthy-looking, even though Mary had never seen a doctor or taken any vitamins during her pregnancy.

At that moment, Mary cries out with tears of sadness, which the doctor and nurses interpret as joy at the birth of a healthy baby. *This moment is supposed to be one of the happiest moments in my life, but my heart is breaking*. It feels like a sharp knife in my heart, and nothing can take that away. She takes a deep, quivering breath and lifts the child to give her to the nurse. Slowly, she turns away while the nurse leaves because, in her mind, she dares not love her.

Mary is exhausted and hungry; she wants to curl up and sleep for a week. Grace rushes in like a child in a giant candy store as she closes her eyes.

"How are you feeling? Is everything OK? Is it a girl or a boy? Is it healthy?"

"Hi, Grace! I'm fine, and it's a girl; she's healthy. You can see her in the nursery." As Grace turns to leave, Mary rolls over and silently sobs.

Grace inches up to the glass, anxious to see her new daughter. She sees her immediately, tightly swaddled in a pink blanket in her little plastic bed. She has a round, angry little face, fiercely crying as if she sensed her future may be jeopardized. Despite her tears, Grace thinks she's the most beautiful baby in the world. She's transfixed outside the nursery window, tears of joy welling at the thought of holding her brand-new daughter. Grace is relieved that this ordeal is finally over. She and Bob are one step closer to starting their family.

Grace returns to Mary's room and says, "Can you ask the nurse to bring the baby in so I can hold her?"

Mary can hardly keep her eyes open. "I'm exhausted right now. Can you give me a little time? When you come back, I'll call the nurse. Could you please pick up Kenny and Kathy and feed them lunch?"

Grace sighs disappointedly, "Sure, I'll see you later."

Mary thought...*Take your time, please*. Mary fell into a deep sleep without realizing it because she was tired from labor and delivery.

Soon after, a nurse awakens her. "Would you like to feed your daughter, Ma'am?"

Turning, she sees the baby in the nurse's arms, sucking hungrily on her finger.

She's a hungry one indeed," the nurse chuckles. "Will you be breastfeeding?"

"No, ma'am, could you please bring me a bottle?"

"Oh. Well, all right then, dear. I'll get a bottle. Hold on."

She places the baby on Mary's lap, "Here she is. I'll be right back."

Mary watches the nurse exit. Mother and daughter are alone for the first time. Mary looks at her baby, squirming in her lap. Suddenly, the baby lets out a familiar wail. *She's so hungry.*

At that moment, Grace enters the room. "You weren't supposed to hold her!"

Mary says, "I'm her mother until I can't be her mother anymore. I can't ignore her while I'm here."

"You're right, Mary. I'm so sorry. It's just that holding your baby will make it so much harder for you. You know that."

Mary gently hands her to Grace as the nurse enters with the bottle. Elizabeth begins to cry. At this moment, Mary wants nothing more than to run away with her new baby and her children, but reality paralyzes her. She tries to rationalize her decision. *This is what's best for her. She'll only have a life of pain with me. People won't understand why she's illegitimate, just that she is. I can't put my family through that humiliation. Besides, what can I provide for her now? Love is not enough to feed and clothe her. Grace will look after and provide for her in ways I can't. It's the only way.*

Mary stays in San Diego for another two weeks while she loses her baby weight and works to save enough to make it back to Chicago. While she teaches Grace how to care for Elizabeth, she cannot help but feel hopeless about changing her situation. Grace tries to bond with her new daughter by cuddling, rocking, and feeding her. It's all Mary can take. She yearns to trade places with Grace, if only for an hour. She has been there too long and doesn't want to leave Elizabeth behind, but she wants to go as quickly as she can before she changes her mind. As Mary packs, she prays for the child she must leave behind and wonders if she will ever see her daughter's rosy cheeks again. *God, please don't let this be it.*

The next afternoon, Mary emerges into a sunny sky, a sharp contrast to her bleak emotions. She loads the car. This is the last day

she will see her baby. She can't speak as she holds back tears.

Grace comes out with the baby in her arms, and Mary asks reluctantly, "Would you like me to drive so you can hold Elizabeth, Grace?"

"No, I'll drive. You can take her."

When they arrived, Grace immediately took the baby back, and Mary got her bags and the kids out of the car. She looks back at Elizabeth, with her bright green eyes and white, blond hair, and wonders what her child will look like as she ages. *What kind of woman will she grow to be? Will she ever know the truth about why I decided to give her up? Will she ever forgive me?* The unrest in Mary's soul was a raging fire burning deep inside. She is grateful for the long trip home. Mary needs time to control her emotions and one day forgive herself.

As Mary and the children take their seats, Mary prays, "God, please help this child forgive me for leaving her behind and watch over her."

Chapter 3: The Trials of Childrearing

It was mid-May of 1956 in San Diego. Salty breezes filled the air, and fluffy white clouds overtook the deep blue sky. Had it not been for Elizabeth being so fussy, Grace would have taken advantage of the beautiful day and gone to the beach. Betty Lee cried often, rarely satisfied, as if she knew something was missing.

In the beginning, Grace coveted the newborn like a bottle of Seagram's Seven; she'd find feelings deep within her to hold and show love and affection toward Betty Lee, but with no maternal instinct, she soon grew tired of the demanding little girl; her constant feedings, nighttime waking, and never-ending diapers.

It wasn't Grace's fault that her childhood in the orphanage had destroyed her ability to conjure up anything more than a superficial love for others.

Grace looked to her neighbors, Cookie and Mrs. Molar, for help when she grew tired of appeasing Betty Lee's needs. Her support system was the only thing that kept Grace's quick temper and frustration at bay.

Bob wasn't due until August, and Grace gradually fell back into her old ways, the bar, her whiskey, and the late nights out. She would often throw parties when Robert was gone, only changing diapers when she had to. Smoke and foul-mouthed sailors filled the room where little Elizabeth lay propped up in the corner like a novelty toy.

Robert arrived back in port late in September 1956. It was a warm, overcast day, and the ocean air flowed through Grace's long, dark hair. As the colossal carrier slowly inched into the pier and docked using enormous ropes, wide eyes glimmered in anticipation, and she could feel her heart pounding. She was anxious for Bob to see her "accomplishment" and praise her for it.

He was back at home port on the USS Essex from East Asia. It was the largest aircraft carrier in the Navy fleet, and Bob was proud to serve his country just as he did during WWII and the Korean wars. His Navy buddies knew him as a hero because he saved the crew of the Essex by dismantling a live bomb that had accidentally fallen off one of the planes as it landed on deck.

Bob never wanted children after his first wife Geraldine cheated on him and got pregnant. When Grace sent him the pictures of little Betty Lee, he quickly changed his mind. He could hardly wait to meet the new addition to his family.

The port was crowded that day, where hundreds of families waited for the crew to disembark the Essex. Grace wore Bob's favorite red dress so he would recognize her in the crowd. He walked proudly down the gangway from the ship with his dress whites pristine. He quickly found Grace and hastily kissed her before his eyes averted to the petite blonde, who was now almost four months old.

Carefully taking her into his arms, he smiled as he looked at Grace and said, "She's so beautiful. I can't believe she's ours."

Excited tears filled his eyes as he stared at his beautiful little girl. He couldn't stop talking about her. Grace, taken aback, wasn't comfortable with only half his attention.

"I have a surprise for you, Bob."

"Oh, what's that?" He asked, his eyes never leaving little Betty Lee.

"I've invited all our friends to come this weekend," Grace said excitedly.

"Honey, do you think that a party would be OK? I mean, what about Betty Lee? What if she gets scared and starts to cry?"

"Oh, Bob, she'll be fine. She loves the attention. Cookie's bringing Nora over, and the Hamilton kids will be here, too. We'll have a fun time. We can't stop living because we have a baby."

Cookie was the nickname given to the little Asian woman who first befriended Grace and helped her most with Betty Lee. She lived beside the base with her husband, Bob's best buddy, Lee Parker. Being the motherly type was in her nature, and Grace could count on her for anything. Cookie had tanned, smooth skin, straight black hair in a bob, and a tiny frame. Despite her four' 9" stature, she could be a real firecracker.

"Alright, honey, let me see if any of my buddies want to come over."

Grace smiled. She was not going to let this baby change her life one bit. To Grace's dismay, most of the party was spent with Bob holding the baby. He didn't let Betty Lee out of sight; every conversation was about her. Unlike Grace, parenthood would come naturally to Bob. He was a proud papa around his friends and shipmates.

Bob remained devoted to Betty Lee as time passed, showering her with attention. There was a tug of war inside Grace's heart and mind between caring for the baby and jealousy over her husband's affection. The father's love for his little girl was forged securely and overshadowed many feelings for his wife. As a result, whenever she was alone with Betty Lee, she had no patience with her. Although Grace never physically hurt her, she often ignored doing what was right when it came to her.

Grace decided it was time to train her to go on the potty at five months old so she wouldn't have to deal with her dirty diaper. She held her arm while she sat on the small potty chair. Elizabeth started crying,

"You go in the potty! Stop crying and go, I'm sick of your crying!"

Elizabeth cried so hard that she fainted on the little potty. Grace panicked, quickly picked up the baby, put her against her shoulder, and patted her firmly on the back. She was relieved when her daughter woke up until Elizabeth resumed her crying. As she often did, Grace put her in a room and let her cry for hours until she got tired and finally went to sleep.

Grace took Betty Lee's bottles several times and threw them away to teach her to hold a cup. She would choke on the liquid because she was too young to understand how to drink from a cup. One day, Bob caught Grace walking in from work to hear Betty Lee crying for her bottle. He saw her struggling to drink from a cup filled with milk.

"What the hell are you doing? Give that baby her bottle back!" He roared.

"She is getting too old for a bottle and needs to learn to drink from a cup!" answered Grace.

"Are you crazy? She's only five months old. Give back her bottle!"

"I can't. I threw the bottles away." She said. "*God, why do you always*

36

stick up for her?"

Bob shook his head, mumbling obscenities over Grace's stupidity. Grace, though annoyed, put the cup training on hold, at least for another month. Bob always won the discussions, which resulted in him going to the store to buy new bottles for Elizabeth. As the baby got older and became more independent, her cries lessened. On June 21st, 1957, Bob shipped out again for a 2-month tour. During this voyage, Bob decided he missed Betty Lee too much to keep going out for so long. He tried to get orders to stay home for more extended periods.

Betty Lee could distinguish between her mother's malignancy and her father's endearment as time passed. Bob and Grace expected a lot from their daughter for varied reasons. If she didn't do things right the first time, her mother would take that opportunity to stress how she couldn't do anything right. On the other hand, Bob was more supportive and tried to be a mentor, a welcome reprieve from Grace's demeanor.

By age four, her smile had betrayed no hint of the neglect she had endured as a baby in Grace's care. Elizabeth was a happy little girl. With her father's guidance, she learned quickly to be a robust, independent girl.

He believed in hard work and pride of character. Having been raised in Mannington, WV, a small mountain town, his father instilled a strong sense of accomplishment. He'd often repeat his father's words to little Betty, "It's important to have pride in everything you do" and "Whatever you do, it should be done right the first time."

Elizabeth often sensed an emotional tug of war between her parents. Grace was rarely discreet about her feelings, throwing temper tantrums whenever Bob paid more attention to Elizabeth. Family outings became a bitter struggle for control.

On one such outing, Grace could no longer contain her seething jealousy. She snapped when Bob pointed out a dress he wanted to buy for Betty for Easter.

She rolled her eyes and exclaimed, "I don't understand why you spend so much money on her clothes. She's a tomboy, and she's always getting into something."

Bob turned. "That's enough, Grace."

Grace fell silent. Though Bob was easygoing, she knew how to push his buttons. And while it wasn't a good idea to cross him since Betty Lee had come along, Grace often did.

"Well, maybe it wouldn't be so bad if you would teach her how to be a girl instead of a boy."

"I teach her what I know, and you teach her how to be a girl. At least try to be the mother I know you can be."

When he married Grace, Bob knew they would never have children, and with his past, which was fine, but he didn't realize until now that Grace was better off without children. Becoming a mother at forty was a lot to take on, but at 30, Bob had more energy and patience.

Bob grabbed Betty Lees' hand and walked away. He'd said his peace. Grace gritted her teeth and murmured as they walked the aisles.

Elizabeth learned that there was no pleasing to her mother, but she did not quit trying to earn her love. When things got tough, there was always Daddy to soothe her. She felt important and valued when she was with him. But he couldn't replace Elizabeth's intrinsic need to connect with Grace. She refused to give up on her mother.

Chapter 4: Daddy's Little Girl

Good times were abundant when Daddy was home, the picture of the perfect family. Betty Lee watched "Howdy Doody" and "I Love Lucy" on the little round television in the living room while sitting on his lap. Sometimes, the family would join the next-door neighbors on a camping or fishing trip, which she always enjoyed. Nothing compared to one-on-one time with her daddy.

One damp, foggy morning when Betty was 5, Daddy took her deer hunting. Before dawn, they headed into the woods with Lee, Bob's best friend. The dark, peaceful forest was interrupted only by their breath's white wisps and soft steps along the wet ground. Betty Lee was captivated.

After a long walk, Bob bent down to her. "This is where we wait for the deer to come out, but you've gotta be quiet, okay?"

She nodded with wide eyes. The three crouched down in the bushes. Soon, a large eight-point buck cautiously approached the clearing. Betty tugged on her daddy's coat excitedly. Bob looked down at her and put his finger over his lips to quiet her before she could speak. Eagerly, she looked at the buck, sniffing the air and ground. Suddenly, more deer emerged from the trees, following the giant buck. Betty couldn't keep her eyes off the big deer, which she considered the protector of his family. Bob slowly positioned his thirty-ott-six with the high-power scope firmly into his shoulder and put his finger on the trigger. He could see the deer as if it were just past his nose, more than twenty-five yards away. Betty Lee became uneasy; she tried to connect the pieces of what was about to happen. However, she dared not move or interrupt her father.

Suddenly, a shot rang out, startling her so much that she jumped and fell onto her backside on the wet leaves. She looked around wide-eyed to see what had happened while grasping at her dad's arm. She saw the big buck lying in the field but no sign of the others. Whimpering, she asked, "Daddy, why did you shoot the deer? Was it going to hurt us?"

"No, Honey. We came out here to *hunt* deer. You wait for them to walk by, and then you aim your rifle at them and shoot a clean shot to the chest area to kill them quickly," he said proudly. "Ya gotta catch 'em by surprise 'cause they are quick and will bolt out-of-sight. Never shoot at the head because a beautiful eight-point buck like that can be mounted on the wall! But most of all, you want to hit him just right so the shot doesn't ruin the meat." *Meat for who? And why would we want to put a deer on our wall?*

Betty nodded, still confused, watching her dad and Uncle Lee tie a thick rope around the hind legs of the big buck. They threw one end of the rope over a big tree limb, then putting the truck in gear, they gently pulled the deer up so its nose pointed to the ground. Bob took his knife out as he walked toward the deer. He slit the deer's throat with one quick action.

Betty Lee screamed, "What are you doing, Daddy? Please stop."

"It's okay, honey Bob reassured.

Stunned, the child watched as the steamy blood gushed onto the dirt with mounting horror. "This is bleeding out, Betty Lee," her Daddy explained. She turned her face away and started to cry.

"Daddy, I wanna go home. I don't like this."

Bob bent down, removed his bloody gloves, and embraced Elizabeth.

"Punkin',' the deer can't feel anything at all. We're not hurting the deer."

Lee just stood there and gave a faint smile, shaking his head and saying, "Bob, this is no place for a little girl. Heck, I don't even bring my boys out here. Kids her age don't need to experience this. It's too bloody."

"But I want her to feel like she can do anything with her life, Lee. She needs to know her fears, not her abilities will limit her."

She looked up at her dad. Then, in a small voice, she asked, "Why is he bleeding so much?"

"We must let the blood out because we want the meat to taste okay when we get him home. The meat gets bad quickly if we leave any blood in."

The guys sat around drinking coffee from their thermos and talking until the deer bled out, and then her father took the knife and slit the carcass from its belly up to its throat. Vapor burst out from all the organs as they tumbled onto the ground. A pile of sweltering intestines flopped onto the cold, damp bed like a mound of sausages. Elizabeth turned away in disgust.

She struggled to understand, "Why do we want to eat him, Daddy?" Bob bent down again to his little girl and put his hands upon her shoulders.

"This is good meat, Sweetie; it will feed us for a long time."

"Do you remember when Mom killed the chickens for us to eat?" Dad asked.

"I remember seeing Mom cut the head off one of my chickens, and it ran around with its head cut off."

"Well, that is what we had to do to have chicken for dinner. It's just a part of life. We eat meat."

Betty watched intently as her daddy and Uncle Lee dragged the enormous carcass to his truck and strapped it down for the haul home. Blood dripped all over the truck's bed and on the ground. Betty took a deep breath before getting in the cab.

Snuggling up to her dad with his arm around her, he explained that life is not what it seems. You will not want to do many things, but you must do them anyway because that is how you learn. All the way home, she replayed the event in her head. She understood more what her daddy had done each time she went through it.

At the house, Elizabeth hopped out of the truck and ran to the back, where Bob and Lee took the chains off the tailgate to let it down. The deer's head slumped over to the side with its tongue hanging out; they dragged the deer out and placed it on a slab to cut the meat for freezing. The smell of the kill stayed with Elizabeth for the rest of her life. She would never eat venison again.

Growing up so close to Daddy meant that she saw things most little girls didn't. In lots of ways, she was more mature than other girls her age. From bating a hook to fixing lights and plumbing, Betty Lee was a motivated pupil; she loved learning new things by her Daddy's side. She could never have imagined the looming event that would shatter the rest of her life.

It was an unusually chilly January morning in San Diego in 1961 when Elizabeth's life turned upside down. She heard the familiar rattling of milk bottles on the front porch, and Mommy was talking to the man in the white suit who always brought the huge block of ice to the top of the refrigerator. She heard the car start and knew her Daddy was off to work.

The sun had just begun to peek above the horizon. Bob was enjoying the scenic morning drive to the Naval Base. Driving on damp roads past the high median of grass between the lanes of traffic, he noticed the frost glistening. Suddenly, a car flew towards him, turning in mid-air and landing on the roof of his car.

It buckled instantly, the jagged edges cutting into Bob's head. He felt a warm sensation running down his face as he screamed in agony. The metal had split his skull, causing blood to flow into his eyes, temporarily blinding him just before blacking out; he lost control of the car and slid across the breakdown lane with the lady's car atop his.

He awoke in the hospital 5-days later. To the surprise of his doctors, the coma left his memory intact. Losing an incredible amount of blood, He died twice: once when the paramedics got him out of the car and in the ambulance. It was a miracle that Bob had survived the brutal accident, but being coherent was even more incredible.

The painstaking surgery removed portions of his brain and left the surgeons frantically cauterizing arteries, grafting the skin, and sealing damaged nerves. The pain was still severe, even with medications. Bob woke up with a blood-curdling scream that resonated throughout the hospital. Moments later, nurses and doctors flooded the room with intravenous sedatives.

Once Bob stabilized, the doctors met to discuss what to do next. Their worst fear had manifested. He was in unbearable pain from all the nerve endings that struggled to work right again. His condition prompted yet another surgery to cut some nerves in the pain center of his brain. Doctors were unsure about how it would affect him when he awoke again.

About two weeks later, Bob left the hospital with a bone graph in his head and what the hospital described as minimal pain.

When he entered the door, Betty looked up in surprise, "Daddy! What happened to your head? Are you ok? I missed you."

Bob wanted to scoop his little girl up, but the pain in his head was too immense. Instead, he looked at her and forced a smile.

"Daddy's fine, Punkin." He looked at Grace standing in the kitchen doorway. "You didn't tell her?"

Defensively, Grace replied, "Well, I figured it would be too hard on her. How do you tell a five-year-old that her daddy had an accident? She wouldn't understand anyway; it would only confuse her."

She ran to her daddy and wrapped her arms around his leg. *"Something's wrong with Daddy! What's wrong with Daddy?* Bob shook his head at Grace and patted Betty Lee on the head, pulling away from her, then went to lie down. Usually, when he came through the door, she could expect a big bear hug and a smile, but now her daddy seemed distant and almost cold. Hurt and confused, Betty Lee retreated to her room.

The loving atmosphere that Daddy had provided over the years never entirely returned. The incident almost claimed his life and left him irreparably damaged. His bright outlook, admiration, and affection for his daughter never fully returned. Bob was often solemn and rarely played with Betty. His loving arms were still there at times, but she quickly learned that her daddy wasn't the same man he'd been.

His temper was shorter, and his anger scared her. He destroyed her bike when she fell off and scraped her knees and elbow. Elizabeth has never seen her father in such a rage. She was afraid to go to him when she thought he would get upset.

Though Betty Lee didn't know the specifics, she knew about her dad's surgery. She wondered what those doctors had removed that had left him so much colder.

Chapter 5: Relation Revelation
Abducting Elizabeth

In May 1961, Mary's nosey younger sister, Betty, unexpectedly visited. Grace was oblivious to Betty's threat and welcomed her openly.

"Betty, this is our daughter, Elizabeth Lee."

"Hello, Elizabeth, that's my name too; nice to meet you," she said, mesmerized by the child's green eyes.

The familiar young face struck Betty, but she couldn't figure out why. She shook her head and looked back up at Grace. "Hey, thanks so much for letting me stay for a while. Where do you want me to put my things?" Betty Lee watched Grace lead Betty into the back bedroom. They had much to discuss, and another party was only hours away. Her mother was an excellent host, using any occasion as an excuse to throw a party. Elizabeth hated her parent's stupid parties: the foul stench of whiskey, the drunken men, the constant cigarette smoke, but she had mastered the art of being invisible.

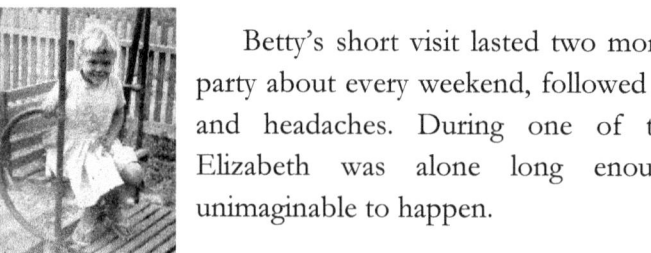

Betty's short visit lasted two months. It was a party about every weekend, followed by hangovers and headaches. During one of these parties, Elizabeth was alone long enough for the unimaginable to happen.

There were times when Grace passed out on the couch, and Betty would have to make the child something to eat because no one else would.

The more time Betty spent with Elizabeth, the more she

understood something was amiss. She found herself staring at the child whenever she came into the room. *Why did Mary leave so suddenly while Grace produced her baby? Why didn't Grace want to be close to her?* Suddenly, it hit her. "Of course! That's it!" *This wasn't Grace's child! She couldn't have children!*

"So, the only option is" *yes, the child must be Mary's,* but *who was the father, and how did Mary hide the pregnancy for so long?*

When Grace rolled herself out of bed and wobbled her way into the kitchen, Betty was there to meet her.

"Hello, Grace, got some get up and go for Ya," Betty said, handing Grace a cup of coffee and a cigarette.

"Oh, thank you. You read my mind."

"Well, you can't live with someone day in and day out and not know what gets them going."

Grace looked at her with a sarcastic smile and shuffled over to the kitchen table.

Elizabeth came out to the kitchen and whined, "Mommy, I'm hungry."

Grace peered up from her coffee and sighed.

"Here, Grace, let me get her a bit of cereal. Don't worry about getting up."

"Thanks, Betty, my head is spinning this morning."

Betty put the cereal down on the living room coffee table for Elizabeth. She bent down and ran her fingers through Betty Lee's hair before returning to the kitchen with Grace.

"It must be tough taking care of such a demanding child when you work so hard. You barely have time to relax and take time for yourself. How do you do it?" Grace stared into her hot coffee, breathing in the steam.

"I get help from the neighbors. Sometimes it's just too much to cope with."

"Did you always want to have children?"

"Bob and I never really wanted children at first," Grace explained, "But we immediately fell in love with Betty Lee. I don't know what we'd do without her. Although, I thought it was going to be different. I wasn't ready for all the dirty diapers and bottle feedings and crying whenever she wanted attention, which seemed to be constantly."

"Mary must have helped you while she was here. She always had that maternal instinct. It must have been a comfort of sorts, right?"

"Sometimes she was depressed. You know…her marriage…"

"That's strange. Mary works hard but likes a good party now and then."

Grace tried to change the subject. "Betty Lee, try not to get any milk on the floor, or you'll be cleaning it up." Elizabeth nodded her head as she sipped the milk from her cereal bowl.

"Don't you think she looks like Kenny in the face? They could've been twins if you look at their childhood pictures."

Uneasy, Grace stood and walked to the coffee pot. "Yea, but she looks exactly like I did as a child. Coffee, Betty?"

"No thanks," she said, staring at the little girl. "Grace, are you sure there is nothing you want to tell me about Elizabeth?"

Grace put her coffee cup firmly down on the table and turned around. "What! What are you talking about?"

Betty got up and grabbed a basket of her line-dried clothes.

"Come on, Grace, you can't have any kids. Myrtle told me about your surgery years ago. You can tell me; I won't say anything."

Grace looked sharply at Betty, "Honestly, I don't know what the hell you are talking about. Who could dream up such a crazy thing?"

"I know Mary has done stupid things in her life, and it wouldn't surprise me if she gave you this baby to hide her mistake. Everyone knows she and Robert weren't together because he was in the Looney Bin."

"Look, that is my child in there! I fed her, clothed her, woke up with her every four hours, and tried to rock her when she just wouldn't shut up! She's mine, Betty, and no one will say different."

"OOOH, you are just as stubborn as Myrtle." Betty huffed as she stomped out of the room. *That little girl is Mary's. Grace doesn't deserve her. I'm much more deserving of Elizabeth than Grace is. Yeah, I should take her with me when I go. I could give her a much better life than these two ever could.*

Elizabeth shuffled back into the kitchen with her empty bowl, "Mommy, can I play with Nora now?"

Grace stared at her and said, "First, you put your bowl in the sink; then, you can go out but stay in the yard."

She skipped outside to play with her best friend as Bob entered the kitchen.

Grace waited for him to sit down before she whispered, "Bob, Betty was asking many questions this morning about who Betty Lee belongs to."

"What are you talking about?"

"She said that she looks just like Kenny."

"So," said Bob, shrugging his shoulders.

"So, she also knows about the hysterectomy."

Bob looked up. "How?"

"She said she overheard her mother talking about it."

"Oooh, Myrtle, she just can't keep her mouth shut; she's always got to be in someone's business." Bob looked back down to his coffee. "She can't prove anything."

"She knows Mary was here when I was supposed to have the baby. She's not gonna give up till she finds out for sure. We should ask her to leave before she blabs to Mary and gets her all stirred up."

Bob was getting more frustrated by the second. "Where is Betty?"

"She's in the bedroom."

He stood up, pushed the chair against the wall, and stormed out of the kitchen. He found Betty putting her laundry away.

"There's no need to put those things away. We want you to leave as soon as you can get a ticket for the train."

Betty looked up wide-eyed at Bob standing in the doorway and said, "Excuse me?"

"We don't have to take any of your shit, and we don't have to explain anything about our daughter, but if you must know, we adopted her. Grace doesn't want anyone to know about it. I think it's time for you to go back to Chicago."

"Is that how it's gonna be? Ok, fine. I'll pack up and leave on the first train out in the morning." Betty knew he was lying. She had to find Mary and confront her.

In the morning, Bob was out the door before sunrise. Betty came out with her things just after he left the house and met Grace in the hallway.

"I just wanted to let you know...I *will* find out about Elizabeth. Something is not right here, and I will find the truth. If this child belongs to Mary, I will tell her how you've neglected her. She'd never approve of how you've been raising her child."

Grace interrupted, "Elizabeth is ours. I told you before you're not thinking straight. It's time for you to leave now. You're not welcome here anymore."

Betty picked up her stuff and slammed the screen door, hitting the wall.

"You don't have to worry about me returning here, but I promise you, it's not over," she said as she got into the cab.

That night, when Bob came home, Grace told him what happened.

"What are we going to do?"

"Well, my supervisor asked me, after the accident, if I wanted to ship over with the Essex, but I didn't want to move, and until now, I had no reason to, but now I have no choice. I'll take him up on that transfer to Rhode Island. I've been working a desk job since Essex left port. I'll be happier doing what I love anyway."

"Rhode Island! Are you crazy? We're established here. In five years, you'll be retiring! How can you think about uprooting us to another base? We have friends here, Bob."

Bob pointed his finger at Grace's face and lowered his voice.

"Listen to me, Grace. No loud-mouthed Bitch is going to take Betty Lee away from us! She is ours; we've come to love her like our own. I'm not taking a chance that Mary might decide she made the wrong decision leaving her with us."

"But Bob, you can't seriously believe she'd come down here to get her daughter after five years."

"I told you, I'm not takin' any chances. Tomorrow, I'll start the paperwork for the transfer. I'll tell them I need to be closer to my father in West Virginia, and then I'll take time off to get our things packed."

Betty finally arrived back in Chicago. When the train stopped, she rushed to the nearest phone booth to call her sister.

With each ring, Betty grew more impatient. On the fifth ring, Mary answered.

"Mary, we need to talk! It's an emergency, and it can't wait!" Her sister's heart was beating fast as she thought of all the possible news Betty had to tell her.

"Well, what is it?"

Betty started again, "No, I can't tell you over the phone. Can I come over right now?"

"I guess. Where are you?"

"I just got off the train from San Diego. I'm on my way!"

She slammed the phone, picked up her bags, and rushed out of the train station. Thirty minutes later, Betty was banging on the door to the little two-bedroom apartment.

Mary's sister was never one to beat around the bush, so she just came out with it, "I met Elizabeth. That child is not Grace's; she's yours, right?"

Mary was stunned. What could she say to that? "I…I'm sorry. Are you out of your mind? What do you mean?" Mary tried to look away from Betty.

"Mary, I know something isn't right. I saw Elizabeth, and she looked just like Kenny when he was younger."

Mary turned around to talk to her sister but could not speak. At that moment, Betty knew she was right.

"Oh, Mary, why didn't you tell me? What happened? Who is the father?"

What was she going to say? She couldn't tell her sister she didn't trust her with such damaging information.

"Calm down, Betty. First, please tell me how Elizabeth is."

"Grace wouldn't admit that she was yours, and Bob said they adopted her, but I didn't believe it for a minute. She said you were depressed, but now I know it was because you were pregnant. Oh my God, how could you give your daughter to a woman without knowing what to do with a child?"

Mary raised an eyebrow, "What do you mean she doesn't know what to do with her?"

Betty put her hand on Mary's shoulder, "You have no idea what kind of person you left her with."

Mary sat down hard on a nearby chair. She felt weak as she stared into the living room…*What have I done? She told me she would care for her as if she were her own. Oh, how could I have been so stupid? I knew Grace had issues, but I hoped it would be different after Elizabeth was born. What was I thinking? I should tell Buck. He can help; I know he can!*

Betty continued, "Grace is selfish, and Bob is always at work. While I was there, they had parties all the time. Grace thought Elizabeth was constantly being a nuisance because she was hungry or scared and needed someone to care for her. Don't get me wrong, they gave her many toys and frilly dresses but neglected her while I was there. You must wonder if the child even gets as much food as she needs. Grace sent her to the neighbor's house countless times to play all day."

Betty paused long enough to ask Mary, "Tell me how all this happened?" I want to help you get Elizabeth back, but I can't if I don't know why you did it. We don't always get along, but you are my sister."

Mary was shocked. This was the first time she thought her sister was being sincere. She took a deep breath and said, "Betty, you are wrong. She isn't mine. It's true. Bob told you the truth; they would adopt her and wanted me to help her because Grace didn't know what to do with a baby.

"Betty, what am I going to do? I can't leave her there; I should get and raise her as my own, but what if Buck won't accept her?"

"It's okay, Mary. We'll get her, and I'll take her if Buck doesn't want her. She's such a beautiful child and so quiet. It would be best if you talked to Buck. He loves you and the kids, and I know he'll understand. Just tell him what happened when you were there, and I'll back you up."

Though Betty tried to empower her sister to move to action, Mary struggled daily as she thought about the consequences she would face if she told Buck the truth. She wanted to ensure that she was doing the right thing and that the circumstances were right before she brought shame and judgment upon herself. Unfortunately, this delay gave Bob and Grace time to disappear.

Part 2: Settling on Shaky Ground

Chapter 6: Big Bugs and New Friends

"Daddy, why do we have to leave now?"

"It's an adventure. We are going to have so much fun, Punkin."

"I'm having fun *here*. Can't we stay here with all my friends and my new school?"

"Honey, listen to Daddy carefully. Your mommy and I love you very much. We would not let anything ever happen to you. You're going to make new friends and have a new home. We can't stay here." Elizabeth started sobbing silently as her dad went on. "My ship, the Essex, has left, and the Navy permitted me to join my crew. We have to leave, but how would you like to help Daddy build a house on the truck?"

"But where are we going?"

"Rhode Island. You'll love it. They've got beaches just as beautiful as San Diego's. First, though, we need to prepare the truck. Rhode Island is on the other side of the country."

Dad and Betty Lee worked for a solid week building a homemade shelter of half an inch of plywood and angle iron atop a White 1955 Dodge truck they lovingly came to know as "Casper." Her daddy explained that angle iron was used to fasten the plywood onto each side, then riveted and drilled holes for thousands of nuts and bolts set two inches apart. The truck itself would fall apart long before the camper ever would. The trailer was in "tip-top shape." He mounted a full-size feather bed on an angle iron in the front of the camper, next to the window just behind the cab seat. When Casper was finished, Betty's favorite place was rolling in the bed and watching where they were going through the window.

The Navy sent the movers to pick up their things the second week of September 1961. They carefully wrapped and packed everything in large boxes, then loaded them into a big truck. Mom packed food, clothes, and cooking stuff into the camper for the next couple of days, and they were on an adventure across the United States. We cooked the venison and snake Dad killed over the Coleman stove and an open fire on our way to Grampa's house.

Six days later, we drove through the narrow tree-lined mountain roads leading up to Grandpa's in Mannington, WV. As I looked out the camper's window, there was a mist wafting up from a bottomless valley below. You could see a faint rainbow in the fog while clouds swirled around the mountaintops. Thick white fog hovered over the brick streets, still wet from the morning dew. Grandpa lived next to the railroad tracks upstairs from the only bar in town.

Grandpa's apartment smelled of grease, beer, and smoke. Behind the stove, the walls were covered with syrupy yellow stuff. Sticky fly paper hung from the ceilings, and dead flies were still on it. The outhouse was out back beyond the gravel parking lot.

Every night for the next two weeks, Mom and Dad were downstairs with Grandpa drinking while I stayed upstairs with the other residents. Lying on a mattress on the floor, watching shadows dance on the ceilings, I felt the vibrations from the loud music. Suddenly, I saw a big black bug scurry across the floor, then another. What is that? I thought. "Daddy," I whispered to myself. "Daddy, where are you?" I pulled the blanket over my face and eventually fell asleep.

BANG! I awoke to a loud noise and saw bugs crawling on me; I threw my blankets off, jumped up, and ran screaming down the stairs.

Crunch, crunch…Stepping on the bugs as I crossed the floor.

"Daddy, daddy, where are you?"

"Betty Lee, is that you?"

"Mommy, big bugs are crawling all over me."

"Stop it now and get your butt back upstairs. You can't be down here."

"But, Mommy, the bugs were crawling all over me."

"Take a shoe and kill them."

"What's going on here, Punkin? Why aren't you upstairs sleeping?"

"Daddy, I can't sleep because of the bugs; there are lots of bugs."

Daddy took me up into his arms and carried me up the stairs. He put the light on in the kitchen and tucked me tight like a mummy. I finally fell asleep again.

Every day, we had new adventures in the woods, unique sights in town, and new people to meet. Plus, I loved how my grandpa gave big bear hugs because it reminded me of my Daddy's hugs.

The day finally arrived when Daddy packed up Casper for our trip to Rhode Island. I was happy to leave those bugs behind but sad to leave my grandpa. It was very chilly outside that night in October, and Mom wrapped me up in a thick blanket and laid me down on the front seat of the warm cab with Daddy. She climbed into the camper to sleep until it was her turn to drive.

Sometime during our two-day trip, Mom and Dad told me not to tell anyone who I was. As Mom explained, I got more confused. She asked, "Do you know why I tell you not to tell anyone we adopted you?"

"No, what does adoption mean?"

"Well, Betty Lee, we are not your natural parents but love you so much. When children are adopted, it's because they are so loved, which makes them so special."

"So why can't I tell anyone?"

"Because we want you to feel like you belong, and if the other kids know you were adopted, they may not accept you. We've loved you as our own since the day I carried you down the hospital steps."

I wasn't sure what to think, but I knew I didn't want to be taken away or shunned by my friends because I was different, so I never considered it necessary.

As we drove along the scenic route that ran parallel to the ocean in Rhode Island, all thoughts of San Diego were soon gone. Before me lay an ocean, the color of the bluest blue in my crayon box. I saw small white ripples swirling along the beach. The small waves couldn't hold a candle to the tumultuous California waves, yet they were beautiful. Large gray boulders lay scattered about along the coast while tall brown and green grasses jutted from dozens of dunes. Rhode Island was breathtaking.

Nature was integrated with life here. Fertile green foliage twisted itself around lush trees all along the road. The rock walls built by Native peoples around the 1600s once separated farmlands but now guard spacious castle-like houses. They must have meticulously handpicked each rock to fit flawlessly into place without any cement.

It was so beautiful. Mom insisted we live in town, but Dad said we would have to live on base until we found a place. Base housing was dreary, flat, brown single-story homes fused all in a row, separated only by a slab of cement in front of each door. The inside was just as cramped. Windows were few, though there wasn't much of a view.

Luckily, Mom soon found a place for rent on Kingstown Road, three blocks from the ocean in Narragansett. Our apartment was on the first floor of an old Grey three-story house surrounded by hedges called 'The Haven House.' It was a grand old place with a deep front yard shaded by an enormous oak. It had a long-paved walkway leading to six wooden steps at the front door. *Memories of my Red Flyer wagon, playing tea with my dolls, and roller skating on the broken sidewalk still run through my mind.*

After unpacking my last doll, I ventured outside and sat on the front stoop.

"Hello, who ah you?" asked a stocky girl with short, wavy blond hair as she flew down the stairs.

"I'm Elizabeth Lee, but you can call me Betty Lee. I live here now; we just moved in. What's your name?"

"Debbie Barber. Waya did you come from?"

"California. Which floor do you live on?" As I thought about how strange her language was.

"We live on the top floa."

"Do you have any brothers or sisters?"

"Yep. I have two brothas. Russell is ten, and Roy is nine. How old ah you?"

"I just turned five in April; I'm going into kindergarten. How old are you?"

"I turned seven in Septemba. Do you know anyone hea yet?"

"No, I had to help my mom and Dad unpack our stuff."

"Would you like to be my friend? I know a few kids around hea, like Joyce. She's a twin, and she has lots of brothas and sistas. She's quiet, but I like her. She's only six, her birthday was in August, but she's smalla than you, and she has freckles all ova."

"Where does she live?"

"She lives on Brown Street." pointing behind the house. "It's on the next street."

"Wow, that's close. Do you think we can go over now?"

"No, we have to be caful cause her mom and her sista Barbara are mean, and she has chores to do every day."

"Really?"

"OH yeah, Tha's six kids in the Brindamour family. Joyce has three sistas: Barbara, Susan, and Nancy. All three of her sistas are older. She has two brothas, too. Alan is the oldest, and Jimmy is her twin brotha."

"That's so cool! Does she look like Jimmy?"

"No, he hasn't as many freckles, but he's got big ee'as," she said as she pointed to her ears.

"Debbie!" I heard from the top of the stairs. "Debbie, get up hea now."

"Bye. Will I see ya later?" asked Betty Lee.

"Shua, I'll be right back; I just have to do somethin for my mom."

As Debbie ran up the stairs, her two brothers came down. Russell is the oldest, with his long blond hair curling around the bottom of his ears. Roy, however, is stocky but has blond hair and blue eyes, just like Debbie.

I started kindergarten a week after moving into my new house. That first day was terrifying.

"Mommy, I don't like this place. It's scary. Look how big it is?"

"It'll be ok. It's tall like that so everyone will fit inside. Come on now, let's go in and meet your new teacher."

As we walk up the long walkway, the tall brick, pyramid-like structure casts a shadow over the entire playground. I waited in the hall while Mom went into the office.

"Okay, Betty Lee, let's go now. Take my hand." Mom said as she led me down the wide, well-worn wooden stairs into the basement. As we came to the second door on the left, I heard children inside laughing and singing to the music on the record player. Mom knocked on the door.

"Hello, come in. You must be Elizabeth." The tall, pretty lady said as she bent down to me.

"Hello," I said as I looked around the room. Everyone had stopped what they were doing and looked at me. Letting go of Mom's hand; I stepped forward slightly as she said.

"Hello, Mrs. Cullen. My name is Grace Ott, and this is Elizabeth."

"Yes, welcome to Rhode Island. Class, Elizabeth is from California. Say hi to her."

"Hello, Elizabeth." The class said in unison.

I loved Mrs. Cullen; she gave us cookies and milk before we napped. I met Joyce and her brother on the playground and realized they were in class with me.

Debbie, Joyce, Jimmy, and I were all walkers. We only had five blocks to walk, but we found many things to discuss throughout the year, mostly our misadventures.

When Debbie was sick one morning, I learned much about her family.

Joyce asked, "Have you met Debbie's Mom yet?"

Looking over at Joyce, who was walking on the other side of Jimmy, I said, "No, but I saw her one day when she was yelling at Debbie. Is she always that mean?"

Jimmy interrupts, saying, "Yah, she's terrible, and I'm glad she's not my mom."

"Isn't she fat? My brotha is as tall as she is," Joyce said.

"Oh, and Roy is mean too. Did you know he hits all the otha kids and yanks off butterfly wings? He was caught shooting cats, and otha animals with his be-be gun, and his mom beat him."

Roy had an affliction for the macabre and could always find a way to horrify me. He was in third grade, so avoiding him wasn't hard.

When Joyce was playing with dolls and Debbie had chores after school, Jimmy and I played with cars under his tree on Brown Street. We made whole communities in the dirt where we lost track of time.

We talked about our chores and California. Sometimes, he would come to my house and offer to help me mow the grass or clean my room. At times, he could be so much fun; other times, he was an absolute jerk, and Mom said it was because he liked me. The boys are so weird.

Jimmy asked, "Do you rememba that day we all tore up the big wicka chai on the front landing of the Haven House?"

"Yeah, we all got in trouble when Dad came home from the base and came after all of us with that old brown slipper."

"He wasn't as bad as yoa mom chasing us around the yawd with that plastic belt. She waved that thing around like a crazy woman trying to run all of us down in foa different directions."

"That was so funny," I said, laughing.

On the playground in the morning before school, Debbie, Joyce, and I hung out in the corner.

Debbie said, "I hate it when our Mothas go out and leave us with Susan. She's mean, just like my mom."

Yeah, said Joyce, "I hate my sista because she's so bossy, and she doesn't have ta do nothin when she babysits us."

I said, "Hey, do you guys remember the night they all played Pinnacle upstairs in your house, Debbie?"

"Yeah, Debbie said. "What about it?"

"Susan got in trouble for not watching us, and we ran up and down the halls until Dad got out his slipper."

"Yeah, that was so cool," Joyce said.

"Yeah, you would think so because you didn't get hit like the rest of us because you were so little and fragile," Debbie said sarcastically.

"It's not my fault I'm always sick. I can't help it." Joyce said with tears in her eyes.

Feeling uncomfortable with her feelings, Debbie changed the subject.

Debbie asked, "Hey Betty Lee, I'll bet you don't go to the dump anymoa with just your flip-flops on?"

"No, my foot still hurts from that broken Coke bottle I stepped on."

Joyce asked, "How many stitches did you get?"

"I got five right there," I said, pointing to my right foot.

"Yeah, that happened right before she got in trouble for losing her mom's hernia clips," Debbie said. All of us started laughing.

"But I'll bet you didn't think it was funny when that Garden snake bit you when you tried to catch it by the tail," Debbie said as she laughed.

"That wasn't funny, Debbie; I didn't know what kind of snake that was. My Dad was so mad that he raced to the hospital to find out it wasn't poisonous."

"You are always getting into trouble, Betty Lee. You've had mowa problems than my brotha, and he's a boy."

"I have fun, and I'm not afraid of anything! My Mom and Dad took me places, and Dad taught me I could do anything If I wanted to. Mom says I'm a Tomboy, but I don't care."

But as tough as I try to be on the outside, some things still make me sad, like thinking about Mrs. Borden.

Old Lady Borden was a fragile but sweet woman with short, wavy white hair. Her arms showed age spots dotted in big splotches. Also, she lived in a small two-room apartment at the back of our building. Joyce and I enjoyed going to her apartment to play with her yellow parakeet, Pauli. I liked to help water her plants in the one west-facing window she had. It was always hot there. The other kids called her names, but I think it's because they didn't know how sweet and caring she was.

I went to see her every day after I left school because Mom and Dad worked until later in the evening. Sometimes, I would sit on the carpet while she braided my hair. She also made the best bologna sandwiches and oatmeal raisin cookies. I would eat while she helped me with my numbers and read fairytales and poetry. Whenever I felt sad, she hugged me and read stories to help me feel better.

Mrs. Borden died before the following Spring in 1962, but I thought she moved. I missed her, and Debbie knew how to ruin my day.

"I'm glad she's dead, and you'll neva see her again."

I yelled at her furiously, "Why are you so mean to me?" I ran to my dad to find out if it was true.

"Daddy, where is Mrs. Borden?"

"Honey, she went to be with the angels. She's happier now."

After school, I still sat on her wooden stairs, thinking about how nice she was and how I wished she were my gramma. I missed her and would sometimes fall asleep sobbing into my pillow. With her death, Mrs. Borden taught me that loss was a part of life.

Joyce missed several school days that year and never seemed to catch up because she was always sick. She was frustrated because she felt like everyone else was more intelligent and physically adept than she was. Joyce also couldn't play sports because of her allergies and asthma. It was a constant reminder that she would never  measure up to the other children. Later in life, not only did it affect her physically, but emotionally and academically as well. In her mind, there was no reason to make goals or aspire to dreams; she had accepted her fate. I felt like she often resented me because I could do many things she couldn't. It was more evident as my life moved forward while hers seemed to creep along.

Chapter 7: The Times They Are a Changing

It was chilly outside in early October 1962, and the leaves transformed into a kaleidoscope of vibrant oranges, reds, and yellows. Dad said it was perfect weather for moving. Mom found a place on Brown Street across from Joyce and packed good ole Casper to move us again.

I wasn't sure I would like it at the new house because we didn't always like each other. It was a love-hate thing. One day, we were best friends; the next, we cut the strings off each other's Chatty Cathy dolls or pulled out her teeth. Being so close to one another, she was hard to avoid. I'd often close myself in my room, listening to music. I don't know what happened, but as time passed, solitude was my only comfort from things I had never noticed before. I wasn't lonely. I just preferred to be alone and didn't know why.

Once we settled into our new apartment, Dad and I found a full-size Brass bed upstairs in the garage. It was my first real bed in Rhode Island, and I loved it. Dad tried extremely hard to make my childhood last. One day, he brought an old wooden Navy-gray bunk bed home for me to paint for my girlfriends to sleep over. We made a hand-carved guard for the top bunk that I painted pink. It was beautiful and gave me a sense of accomplishment.

Mom searched for a new job. I never knew she was such a good cook until she got a job as a cook at a bar called Schillers out in Point Judith. She never really cooked for us at home except for the fried chicken she shook in a paper bag and cooked in Crisco in our cast-iron skillets. Sometimes, she took me with her when she didn't want to pay for a babysitter. Unfortunately, we didn't get home until late. I stayed back in first grade for two reasons: Jimmy harassed me in class, and I didn't get any sleep during the week. When I got sleepy or had a tummy ache from all the Maraschino cherries, she would put me on a cot in the kitchen while she and Dad drank. I was accustomed to sleeping with noise.

Surprisingly, there were benefits to growing up in a bar. I was well-liked; the customers were friendly and gave me quarters for the jukebox. I learned the shimmy, the swim, the twist, the jerk, and the waltz. I learned to play pool by standing on a milk crate and maneuvering around the table. Sometimes, the whiskey smell on Mom made me feel like I would throw up.

I was the only kid in the place until Laddie Winters' Dad started bringing him in to keep me company. He had long blond hair like a girl but always wore dirty clothes and smelled like fish. His Dad was a fisherman down in Point Judith, and Laddie helped him on the boat. We had lots of fun.

One night, Dad got angry at one of the guys. A slow Waltz came on, and a man grabbed me up from the pool table and held me so close to him that dad jumped up from his chair, ran over, took me from him, and punched him in the middle of the floor!

Yelling, Mom said, "What are you doing? Let go of him. Are you crazy? He wasn't doing anything wrong."

I was crying, stunned that Daddy flung me to the floor.

"Don't you ever touch my kid like that again? I'll kill you if I see you looking at her sideways."

Dad was so angry. I never saw him that mad before, not even at Mom. I got off the floor, ran to the back room, and shut myself in the dry food room so no one could find me.

Mom came in and found me crying on the corner floor. She bent down to me to see if I was okay.

"Are you okay, Honey? Are you hurt? What happened? What did that man do?"

Whimpering, I said, "Mommy, I don't know what happened. He just wanted to dance. He squeezed me so tight I could hardly breathe, and his breath stunk."

Daddy returned to the room, rushed past Mom, and picked me up.

"Are you okay? Did I hurt you?"

"No, Daddy, I'm okay. Are you mad at me?"

"No, Punkin, Daddy's mad at Paul. He should know better. He won't be bothering you anymore."

Mom and Dad got drunk again, maybe because of what happened. Dad left the bar first in his car, then after Mom closed Schillers like many nights before, she laid me on the truck seat to sleep and started home. She was a bit drunker than usual because a loud crash awakened me, and the impact jettisoned me into the floorboard, jamming my neck between the gearshift and seat. She had crashed Casper head-on into a giant oak tree. The tree hadn't moved for two hundred years; my drunken mother wouldn't change that.

The police showed up, and a tow truck took Casper away. Thankfully, the police drove us home. I was glad Mom wasn't taking us anywhere for the rest of the night.

Between my aching body, stiff neck, and pounding headache, I could stay home from school, which never happened. Joyce came over right after school to find out why. Mom's accident brought back memories of the day she lost her big brother. I heard that he died but never knew the whole story.

"Ya know, my mom wasn't always so mean. She was nice to us befoa my brotha Danny was killed downtown."

Curiously listening, I asked, "What happened?"

"The summer befoa you got hea, Joyce explained; we used to go to the beach togetha. Susan held Danny's hand, and Nancy held mine and Jimmy's hands when we crossed Pia (Pier) Road because the caas used to speed through theya. We crossed the road, but Danny waited and didn't cross with us. Susan let his hand go. Then, Danny statted across the street in front of a caa that stopped for him, but another car in the otha lane didn't stop, and it hit him. It was horrible. I'll neva forget. He flew up high, and when he came down, he hit the street, and theya was blood everywhya. It was coming out of his nose and eyes."

"Oh my God. What did you do?"

"Susan and Nancy screamed when they saw it and grabbed us to hide our faces, but it was too late. We saw it all. I heard someone say he was dead. I saw him move, so he was alive."

"Did the ambulance come and take him to the hospital?"

"No, they took him to the Police station. We found out lata that he died theya. Mom neva forgave Susan and became very mean after that."

"I'm so sorry you lost him. My neck hurts. Can we talk tomorrow?"

It took me a few days to fully recover from Mom's accident. I was thankful it wasn't worse.

Narragansett winters were so beautiful. The snow was so white that it had a bluish tint reflecting a bright blue sky. It seemed like billows of cotton draped across the rock walls and farm fences. The ice on the bare trees shined like the glitter on a Christmas tree. Snowplows would pile the snow on the sidewalks between the street and the big hedges on our block, saving most of the snow for the corners. With trudging feet, we forged a pathway of compacted snow on our way to the giant white mounds we could burrow through to make our fort. It was time for war against the boys. We carved out ice windows that faced our enemies to throw snow bombs at them.

Our mittens and socks got wet and cold too soon. I wanted to stay out and play, but when we couldn't feel our fingers, we went inside to warm up in front of the open door on the oil stove, where we hung our wet stuff. Sometimes, Mom would make us all a cup of hot cocoa and chicken noodle soup or grilled cheese sandwiches.

There were days when Mom was great and was a happy drunk, except when she wasn't. She had a guitar she would play for us kids when we asked her to. I remember when Jimmy was with us making fun of Mom for being so drunk; he thought he would be funny. Mom kept a box of Kleenex next to her on the table because she often had a runny nose while trying to sing and play guitar. All of us kids were eating Hostess cupcakes while we listened and sang along with her. Jimmy saw her reaching for a Kleenex and replaced it with a cupcake wrapper. She had cake all over her face and didn't realize it until we told her. Of course, we had to stop laughing first.

Joyce and I were much better friends than Debbie, but sometimes I felt they didn't want me around. Joyce, or Skeeter as I liked to call her because she was small like a mosquito, was easier to hang around with. On the other hand, Debbie was more like me, and we could do more together. Still, she was vindictive, just like her mother, and they often talked behind people's backs, so they were not easy to be around for long. Debbie was the oldest and much bigger and bullied all of us. Her mother, Ginny, said mean things to Joyce and me, which stuck with us for many years. She called me a spoiled brat and told us we would never amount to anything. My mom had a knack for seeking out some of the nastiest characters. They could sometimes make Grace look like a saint, especially when she lets Ginny charge food for her family of four.

Ginny called, "Wheya's your Motha?"

"She's in the bathroom. Can she call you right back?" I asked.

"Betty Lee, listen to me, don't foaget. You neva do what you'a told. Just make shuwa you tell her."

"Okay."

I walked into the other room and called out to Mom, "Mom, Ginny wants you to call her, and I'll bet she needs more food."

"You watch your mouth. Who do you think you are that you can talk about adults that way?"

"She doesn't like me; she's always saying mean things to me."

"That's ridiculous; she's an adult and would never hate a child."

"Yeah, okay," I say under my breath.

Mom and Ginny get off the phone, and Mom says, "C'mon Betty Lee, let's go down to McCullough's Market and pick up food for Ginny and the kids. And I don't want to hear your smart mouth."

"Why can't she go get it?"

"You know she doesn't have a car. How's she supposed to get there? Stop it now."

I bet she wouldn't be so fat if she walked those eight blocks to the store.

Arriving at Ginny's with four bags of groceries she didn't help carry in, I couldn't help but think about all the times she used Mom. Ginny went wherever she needed; she borrowed money she never paid back and treated me like dirt.

"Here ya go, Ginny," hoping to get a thank you, but no, she gave me the same "I hate you" look while she hugged Mom.

We'd been in Rhode Island for under three years and were about to take a trip around the Great Lakes to see Mom's side of the family.

Mom said three days before our trip, "There is no need to tell the family we adopted you. It never happened. Just forget about it."

"Why would I say anything? I know the rules; I know I'm not supposed to tell anyone," I said, realizing my mother didn't trust me.

"Just don't mention to any of our family that you were adopted."

Dad told Mom to shut up, "You didn't have to bring that up. What is wrong with you? He repeated it, "Why would you bring that up?"

"Come on, Bob. I've always told her she was adopted. This is nothing new; she's old enough to understand that."

Dad just shook his head and walked away while she continued.

Grace would sometimes say strange, inappropriate things to me for no reason. She would come into my room and wake me on a few occasions. She'd sit next to me on my bed, sometimes pushing me over to get comfortable, and with slurred speech and whiskey, tell me never to let little boys touch me "down there." I tried to pretend to be asleep, but she pushed me awake and breathed in my face. I had no idea what she was talking about at the age of eight, but I quickly learned the day Jimmy took what didn't belong to him and violated a trusted friendship.

On warmer nights in the summer, Joyce and I would make tents out of old blankets draped over chairs on the front porch and sleep in them all night. It was our version of camping without our parents. During one of these outings, I suddenly awoke from a dead sleep to find Jimmy's hand down my pants. I couldn't believe it. I was horrified at the fact that someone who was like my brother would touch me there. I couldn't even imagine why he would do it. When he saw me wake up, he quickly took his hand out of my pants as if nothing  had happened and ran back home. What was I going to say? I was in shock. Should I tell someone or keep it to myself and try to forget it? I wrestled with whether to tell his sister. She was my best friend, and she might understand after what we'd been through together. Then I stopped myself. *What if she takes her brother's side? What if she hates me for accusing her brother of such an awful thing? What if she doesn't believe me?* No, I couldn't take the chance. I would try to forget the whole thing that happened, just like the adoption, and make sure it never happened again! I was so angry with him that we didn't play with cars anymore, but I didn't want my relationship with Joyce to be strained. Besides, keeping secrets was something at which I was good.

I started waking with severe chest pains around this time, in the middle of the night, unable to breathe. I had no idea what was happening to me. I was scared. First, my parents thought it was an allergic reaction and that I should stop drinking chocolate milk. Later, they thought I just made it up to get attention. Either way, it was never resolved but disappeared after a few months. Thinking back on it, I think it was anxiety.

Dad was dealing with challenges of his own. In 1965, he retired from the Navy. It should've been a time of rest and retirement, but Mom kept him working with all the tabs she continued to rack up. He was under so much stress, but the money the Navy gave him for retirement was insufficient to cover all the bills. She was slowly driving him into the ground daily, nagging and fighting about everything he said or did.

Defiance and opposition can wear a person down after a while. They die from a lifetime of stress, get divorced from the problem, or eventually, give in to it and accept that they'll never be happy. It's not good for two eternally obstinate people to live in the same house together. I've learned two things over the years: you must pick your battles or be ready to lose the war, and no relationship is worth being miserable because life is too short.

Chapter 8: A Fleeting Childhood

I rarely saw my parents affectionate and certainly not with me. Not only was there no intimate talk between them, but they also slept in different beds, seldom kissed, and rarely said a sweet word to one another. Until age seven, I thought it was normal for parents not to say they love you.

My Dad knew I needed him to take away my hurts and make me stand tall when I felt like no one loved me. I wasn't the one draining him dry emotionally, physically, and financially, so it wasn't hard for him to spend time with me. He wanted to teach me things because he knew how eager I was to learn. I was his little girl, auto apprentice, and home-fixing helper. I might have turned out much differently without my Daddy's guidance.

In third grade, at age nine, Jimmy would constantly torment me and cause me to yell at him, so I was always in trouble for "acting out," but academically, I was ahead. Dad helped me make a timestable chart to study for the back of my door. I was already ahead of Joyce in school. Mom and Dad bought Dr. Seuss books and encouraged my reading. By age ten, I could read like a sixth grader. My parents only had a ninth-grade education. When she had been drinking, Mom used to make me read aloud to Joyce, and in her typically cruel fashion, she'd often quip,

"See there, how well she reads? How come you can't read like that? Are you stupid?" She never realized her family was too poor to get books.

I know it made Joyce feel bad when Mom compared me to her, but as much as I protested, it didn't do any good. Mom's taunting only added to Joyce's ever-growing resentment of me because she felt like I was trying to be better. Still, all I ever wanted was a couple of good friends to go out and play with. It wasn't all bad as we had great moments.

Picture this: me, almost nine, Debbie, eleven, and Joyce, nine, are sleeping over on a Summer Friday night. We're all excited that summer has finally arrived. Debbie gets the big brass bed because she's bigger than Joyce and me. Joyce wanted to sleep on the top bunk, so I took the bottom. After an hour of teasing, laughing, and carrying on like little girls often do, we decided we wanted something to eat.

Dad had come home from the night shift at 11 p.m., and he'd been in here twice in his underwear, already telling us to be quiet. Dad didn't care who came over. He wasn't putting any pants on if he didn't want to.

Joyce said, "I'm hungry. Can we make a sandwich?"

"Sure. I want one, too."

"Not me," Deb said.

We got up quietly, and Joyce made her peanut butter and jelly while I made a bologna sandwich. We ran, got back into bed, and then got loud again.

Thump, thump, thump. It sounded like the giant in "Jack and the Beanstalk" was coming towards the bedroom door. Suddenly, the door swung open, and a giant silhouette stood there.

"I told you to stop making so much noise. Now, this is your last warning. If I must come in again, I'm warming some butts."

We all hid our sandwiches and our heads under the covers as we giggled.

"I mean it, Betty Lee, you listenin to me?"

"Yes, Daddy."

After he returns to bed, I eat my sandwich, pushing up Joyce's mattress with my feet. She's flying up there telling me to stop in a whisper, then suddenly.

"Stop, Betty Lee," she says in a scream.

Here comes the giant again, but this time, he slams the door open, sees me on the bottom bunk, yanks me out of bed, and spanks me with his slipper. Deb is laughing under the blankets, and Joyce hides her head. Then, Dad pulls off the top bunk guard and throws it on the floor.

"Joyce, come over here." Dad reaches across the top bunk, but instead of getting Joyce, he grabs her sandwich and throws it out the door.

Joyce got one little pat on her butt, then he left, saying, "Now get out of that bunk and clean up this mess." Dad said as he went back to bed.

Joyce said, "I'm not cleanin it up. It was your fault. You kicked my mattress."

"Well, I'm not cleaning it up alone because you yelled."

"Okay, let's clean it up, it's not that bad." She said.

Rounding the corner from the bedroom, we cringed when we saw that the little round fan was on in the kitchen, and our fan had no cover. Dad hit that fan square in the middle, and there was peanut butter and jelly everywhere. It was on the walls, the refrigerator, the floors, the stove, and even Mom's favorite chair.

"Oh my God. We're in lots of trouble."

"How are we gonna get all this stuff up?" Joyce whispered.

"You know where the wash rags are. You could start over there, and I'll start with the fan."

"I'm not doing it. You do it. It wasn't my fault."

I couldn't yell and didn't want another spanking from Dad, so I cleaned it up myself. There was no peanut butter or jelly when Mom got home from the bar. I didn't talk to Joyce for a week after that, but our love-hate relationship soon turned on again.

One of my childhood's greatest and most incredible memories was how Dad was a surrogate father to my girlfriends. He was good at taking his three girls to the movies with enough money for a big bucket of popcorn and a pack of Raisenettes. It was right across the street from the bar, where we'd all get one dollar's worth of penny candy after the show. I ate so much candy my belly would hurt, but I remember laughing and having so much fun. I would regret what that candy did to my teeth later.

The summer I turned nine, Joyce was still living across the street from us, and not a day went by we didn't see each other. The only problem was that her mother got her up at the break of dawn to do chores, and I was always a night person.

"Hey, Betty, wake up. It's Saturday!" Joyce said as I rolled over in bed to find her standing there. *I wish Mom and Dad wouldn't always leave the door unlocked.*

"Let's do something, sleepy head. How can you sleep all day?"

All I wanted to do was curl up in my newly painted purple room and my new bedroom set with a matching dresser and desk with my record player.

"The weekend is the only time I can sleep in. What do you want?"

"C'mon, get up, let's go, get dressed." She said, pulling the blankets off me.

"Alright, gimmie a second."

I yanked on my jeans, brushed my teeth, and we left out the front door past Mom, still passed out in her bed in the living room.

Hindsight and all that, I should've stayed in bed.

Joyce jumped at the opportunity to escape her overbearing family and the mounting chores she had to do every day. She often put a fire under my ass when I was too depressed to go anywhere, and for that, I will always be grateful. We had no one else to care for us, so you might say we raised each other.

With nothing else to do in a small one-horse town, we headed to the beach for a few hours and sat on the seawall. We stopped in Bernice's for a soda, came back toward the house, and went to our friend's house on Caswell Street, where that beautiful, massive, soon-to-be-infamous weeping willow tree stood.

"Hey Betty, bet you can't climb higher than me?" Johnny said, yelling down from the tree.

"Watch me." He yelled, jumping up and down on a high branch.

Running to get a head start, I jumped up on the first branch and swung my leg up to get a better grip. Pulling myself up one branch at a time, I eventually reached Johnny.

"I told you I could do it. Watch this." I said as I climbed up two more branches.

"Get down, you're too high." Joyce and the others screamed as I walked out on one of the branches.

Suddenly, I heard a crackling sound, and just then, the branch I stood on snapped under my bouncing weight. I fell, grasping at anything I could while my body flipped over and over. Each time, I hit another branch. My right arm snapped, and then my collarbone and all I could see were flashes of darkness and branches coming at me. It happened so fast I could not tell how hurt I was. I landed on the exact right arm in full force on the ground. The fall tore the ligaments around my breastbone and pushed my broken collarbone out of my flesh, making breathing almost impossible. I lay there on the ground with Joyce, screaming until I blacked out.

I woke up to Joyce and four other kids looking down on me. I was bleeding, and I couldn't breathe. Slowly, I turned over on my side and pushed up with my good arm. The kids started screaming.

"Mom, Dad, hurry, come outside. Betty fell. She's hurt, quick."

I just wanted to go home. Surprisingly, I didn't have much pain and wasn't crying, but I saw my right arm twisted behind my lower back, and I couldn't move it. As I tried to stand up, I found myself lightheaded. Then I noticed the bone sticking out of my flesh. *Oh my God. What have I done? I'm going to die. Was I in shock? Why didn't I panic? There was just a powerful urge to get home.*

Before making it home, I left a trail of fresh blood around the corner, across the street, and down the sidewalk. Joyce slammed open the door and said, "Hurry, Betty fell out of the Walker's tree. She was up high." I limped in, twisted like a pretzel, bleeding all over the floor.

"Betty Lee! What the hell happened to you? Oh my God. Oh my God. What did you do? Oh my God!"

She grabbed my arm and wrapped it in towels. Then, she put me in Casper, with a pillow under my arm to keep it in place and peeled down the street.

"Should I go to the base or South Country Hospital? South County is closer, but...No, we're Navy and can't afford the civilian hospital. Okay, we're going to Quonset Point. How do you feel?"

"Mom, it hurts, it hurts so badly. I can't stand the pain." I black out occasionally. Thinking back now, I realize it was more important for her to save money on a trip that took over an hour instead of a ten-minute drive to South County Hospital.

When we got to Quonset, they informed us that all the surgeons were off for the weekend and that we would have to go to the Newport Naval Hospital.

The trip to Newport was grueling. Every time my shoulder was jarred, a surge of unbelievable pain went through my upper body. We had to take the Newport Ferry across the choppy ocean water, and every time the boat went up and slammed back down, I wanted to die. I was bleeding badly, and my head was getting so light I could hardly move. My breathing was getting increasingly shallow as I struggled to force air through the weight on my chest.

After the thirty-minute ferry ride, we drove another ten minutes to the hospital. They immediately took me to a room, where three doctors started frantically moving around me.

"Hurry, she's lost a lot of blood. Get an x-ray stat."

Another doctor took the towels off the wound and approached me with a large, thick gauze pad to stop the bleeding. He immediately drew back with a wide-eyed look when he applied the pressure.

"Oh shit! We have a problem!" the young intern said.

"Damn," The chief said. "We have an exposed collarbone. It looks like it tore right through the ligaments. It just missed the jugular. She's a lucky kid."

"Probably doesn't feel that way to *her* right now. We will have to sedate her to straighten out that arm."

"No, please don't, please...It hurts, don't touch it. I pleaded as another doctor came at me with a big needle.

"Sweetie, this will help you sleep. It will make you feel better." He walked behind me and gave me a shot in my butt.

Suddenly, I felt warm all over, and as I started to fall over on the table, one of the interns caught me and gently laid me on my left side. The next thing I remember was waking to my screams.

"Stop, stop, no, it hurts, stop."

One doctor held me around my waist to stabilize my body. At the same time, the other grabbed my legs to prevent any movement. The chief snapped my upper arm into place and then positioned my lower arm in front of me. I lost consciousness twice.

The doctors shot another x-ray and gave me another shot. When I left, I was in a heavy upper body cast that started at the mole on my neck and ended just north of my privates. Except for my left arm, I felt like a mummy. They said I fractured my collarbone, broke my upper arm, and tore the ligaments around my breastbone.

For eight long months, I wore that miserable cast. When I washed up, I had to get my mother to wash my legs, feet, and bottom. At nine years old, I wanted my privacy and independence, but I couldn't do the simplest things for myself. If you've ever had an itch you couldn't reach, you know the uncontrollable feeling that drives you crazy. I would poke my head out the door and scream for Joyce across the street, and she would run at top speed with a ruler in hand to help me.

I learned to eat, write, and brush my teeth with my left hand. I was laughed at in school, but I didn't know if it was because I smelled bad or how I walked under the weight of that rigid encasement.

I spent a lot of time in my new Princess canopy bedroom Dad bought me for Christmas. He's been generous since I broke my arm. What else was I able to do except get myself in trouble again?

I started smoking with all my friends because I wanted to be a part of the group, but Joyce didn't care. She couldn't even breathe.

Debbie stole Winston Reds from her brother Russell. I would sneak out late at night with her to the front of the house next door, where we hid on the high back benches surrounded by hedges. When it was dark, no one could tell we were there. I wanted to be cool, but I was afraid to inhale.

Debbie hated that. "You got to inhale it, Betty Lee. Stop wasting the cigarette!"

When I inhaled the swirling grey smoke, it felt like I had just breathed in burning water. They were incredibly harsh cigarettes, and I coughed so hard that I thought I was coughing up a lung and burning up every nose hair. It was painful, but I wanted to be accepted, so I kept on inhaling. Pretty soon, I was hooked.

Sometimes, I stole cigarettes from Mom when she was drunk and wouldn't notice.

My life was changing at an exponential rate. I started my menstrual cycle and wearing a bra. Given a choice, I would've bypassed this time in my life and gone straight to ten. However, the summers we all spent out at Burlingame State Park were times I will never forget. Mom, Ginny, and May were on the lake in a rowboat on one enjoyable trip, and one lost an oar. They were screaming and waving their arms, almost tipping over the boat. The guys had to decide who would save them, so they sent Cecil out with an extra oar. We laughed for many years over that one.

By the time I was ten, life made a little more sense to me. I had time to reflect on my life and the people around me. I learned to hide the feelings I felt when people put me down. Inside, I was hurt, and those feelings came out as rebellion. I wore a mask of deception that made everyone think I was stronger than I was. I learned to accept that acknowledgment and praise would not be as abundant as ridicule and admonishment.

More importantly, I saw Mom and Dad's relationship for what it was. It created a comfort zone for both. Mom didn't leave Dad because he supplied the money for her habits. Dad didn't leave Mom because he would never see me again. They were miserable and stubborn enough to stay that way.

Chapter 9: Adolescent Adjustments

"Can I get you something to drink, Ma'am?"

I saw a pretty, blonde flight attendant smiling at me. Janet, her nametag read.

"Sorry, I was somewhere else. I'll take hot cocoa, thanks."

I watched Janet continue down the aisle, flashing her wide smile at each row of passengers. When she headed back towards the cabin, I returned to the window and allowed myself to drift back to 1966. I turned ten in April and remember that America was whirling from race riots in Atlanta and an earthquake in Turkey that took over 2300 lives. Black Power and the formation of the Black Panthers dominated American politics. Miniskirts were in fashion, and James Bond, 007, was famous on TV. Star Trek's first full-color episode aired, prompting everyone to buy a color TV.

Joyce moved two blocks away to Narragansett Ave. We still spent time together, walking to the beach with my transistor radio, singing "Eleanor Rigby" by the Beatles and "Monday, Monday" by the Mamas and the Papas. I was finally out of the dreaded body cast, and life was starting to look up for a change. Aside from Joyce nearly bleeding to death, we would've had a great summer.

As kids, we always dared each other to do things to test our limits. On our way to the beach one day, we walked past the flagpole in the baseball field at the bottom of Brown Street. I successfully climbed the pole a week earlier when Joyce wasn't with me, but now it was her turn.

"Hey Joyce, bet ya can't climb up and touch the ball on the top of that pole."

"You can't, eitha."

"Oh yes, I can; I did when I was with Debbie."

"I don't believe you. Show me."

So, I did. I climbed up to the top and slid back down.

"Okay, it's your turn."

"Okay, but can you help me get statted?"

"Sure," I said as I helped her up a little.

She shimmied up the pole, slipping as she passed the tie-off point. Her body was dangling from the bar by her upper arm.

Screaming, she said, "Help! Help me, and I can't get down; it hurts!"

"Oh, my God, Joyce, don't move. I'm coming up."

"Hurry, but don't touch me. It hurts."

"How can I get you down if I don't touch you?"

She screamed and cried as we tried to unhook her arm from the tie-down hook.

I boosted my head under her butt, and she came loose from the hook as we fell to the ground. She got fifteen stitches from that one, and it wouldn't be the last time we found ourselves in trouble. I started fifth grade in September. The school we went to was in what they called "The Relocatables." Temporary trailers had to be set up for us 'Baby Boomers' in the Narragansett Jr. High School playground. They had no heat or air conditioning. We went to school in our jackets and mittens during the winter. Sometimes, we could see the steam from our breath. We also had difficulty writing with mittens on our hands.

In the summer, it was like breathing in a tin can. The air was so muggy and hot that we'd sweat all over our papers and through our scant clothes, sticking to our seats with our bare legs. It was hard to concentrate on schoolwork under those conditions.

I butted heads with a bully named Martha Corr. She looked like a boy with short, dirty-blond hair and buck teeth. She called me rude nicknames and yelled at me from across the playground so the other kids would laugh at me. She would tell me I was yellow and a chicken because I was afraid to fight her. I didn't want any trouble like before, so I tried to be the better person and ignored her.

Every day, Martha made me feel inadequate in front of the other kids. She wanted everyone to know that if you weren't her friend, you were her enemy. Regardless, I stuck to my guns, but each day was more challenging. Occasionally, I would come home with my clothes ripped or dirty, and Dad would ask me, "What the hell happened to you?"

I'd put my head down and tell him about Martha.

He'd shake his head and say, "You need to give her a dose of her own medicine. Defend yourself, Punkin."

His words didn't make me feel any better, but Dad wasn't good at pep talks.

Dad worked at the boatyard, where he made fiberglass docks. He'd have to stand in the water to finish creating them. It was a tough job, especially in the winter when the water was icy cold.

He got highly ill from working outside. He hated the hospital and waited almost two months before seeing a doctor. In the meantime, I'd rub medicine called "Heat" into his hairy back to help him breathe and stimulate his muscles. It was tough for him to inhale, so he'd fall asleep sitting up with his head slumped over the side table on his arms. I hated to see him like that.

When Dad started wheezing so he couldn't catch his breath, he finally went to the hospital and found he had developed bilateral pneumonia. He had to stay in bed for almost two months, and I'd rub Heat on his back with an applicator. It was the most challenging thing Dad ever did, except going to war. All his life, he worked hard and kept busy. There was always something to do, but now he had to lie idly by watching TV as thoughts of daily tasks and work drove him crazy.

We spent a lot of time together while Dad was stuck at home. One of our favorite things to discuss was how government policies affected our country. It wasn't unusual, in our house, for Dad and me to disagree over politics. Dad was a Democrat, and I was a Republican. We were constantly arguing about something the government was or wasn't doing. Even at ten and eleven years old, I kept up with all the current events in America.

Dad and I might have had a little trouble seeing eye-to-eye concerning politics. However, I learned a lot from him, and he respected what I had to say. By age twelve, we were closer than ever. Whenever he would work on cars, I was right there with him, getting greasy and learning about engines, transmissions, and how to change the oil. He even taught me how to steer around buoys in our new-to-us twenty-four-foot cabin cruiser, which he bought, and we fixed up together.

We went to the stock car races in Seekonk, MA, once a month and watched the cars slide around the dirt track and get into wrecks. The wire fences were so low that once, a tire came off one of the cars and took a lady's head off, killing her instantly. I was devastated and asked to sit back further from then on. We bet which one we thought would win. I especially loved the hotdogs and being with him.

Our relationship was on a level few girls had with their father, making me feel secure and safe when he wasn't drinking. It annoyed Mom that we got along so well. She thought I was too old to be 'Daddy's little girl,' but Dad would always stick up for me, making me feel better. He was the only person in my life who genuinely believed in me. I can still hear his words ringing true, *"Betty Lee, you can do anything you set your mind to. Don't you ever forget that the only boundaries you have are the ones in your mind!"* I had turned into his little boy rather than his little girl, which was something Mom rubbed in his face every day. He took more of an emotional beating over me than in any other situation. Still, he wouldn't give up on defending me against her.

It wasn't like she was an angel anyway. Mom was having enough trouble keeping her license because she wouldn't stop drinking and driving. She had multiple run-ins with the town officials than anyone else I knew. Consequently, she lost her license for a year after hitting a police squad car with Casper. That was when Casper was pronounced "totaled." The cop car died as well. Dad was not happy with Mom at that point. He refused to buy her a car, so she bought a blue Chevy Nova and drove without a license to get to work. She never stopped drinking and driving. After losing the truck, Dad got a white LTD, a boat on wheels. Mom was set in her ways and wouldn't quit because some cop had taken her driving privileges.

It was peculiar that everyone saw her as an unselfish person who would give them the shirt off her back if it meant helping a neighbor. She had this big facade, which is why my friends liked her so much.

She wasn't fooling Dad or me, though. Mom took Dad's hard-earned money and blew fifty to sixty dollars a month on the Barbers and the Brindamours. It was a lot of money back then, and most of their fights were over that very thing, but Mom didn't care as long as she looked good to them. Dad worked overtime to pay for the tabs she left at McCullough's Market and the gas station. It was a high price to pay to keep up appearances.

In February 1968, in Rhode Island, snow piled on the ground. We all gathered at the skating rink just off the bridle path to our school for hot cocoa while the larger guys in the neighborhood made paths in the snow. My friend Margaret and I loved to skate there, but best of all, Russell was there. He knew I had a crush on him even though I was afraid to tell him or anyone.

This year, I took a corner too sharply and cracked my knee. I was on crutches for four months. The good news was that Russell was my hero, my love.

Joyce lived on Narragansett Avenue for about a year before her father returned from the Merchant Marines; he moved the family into a big house in the country. Mom and Dad took me to see her one weekend. I was happy to see Joyce but anxious to leave. She wasn't the only one excited to see me. Jimmy's eagerness made me wary about staying the night.

That was the night that Jimmy pounced. Like a lion, he waited for me to fall asleep before touching me again. I pushed him away and said loudly, "Get out of here, Jimmy! Leave me alone and get out!" He left quickly, and I saw Joyce had closed her eyes quickly and pretended to be asleep. I knew then that she was aware of what was going on. Was her brother messing with her, too? I couldn't even think about it. Indeed, he wouldn't molest his sister. I didn't go back to sleep. I couldn't. It was the last time I spent the weekend at Joyce's house.

Joyce's father left her mom two years later, and they lost the house when May went on welfare and couldn't make the payments anymore. They moved into an old two-story apartment building in the city. No matter where Joyce lived, I kept in close contact with her, and we continued to hang out.

Growing up, I passed a small white Baptist Church every day on my way to school. I never noticed the little place; there wasn't much to look at, chipped paint and tiny windows. Then I saw her. She was leaving the church, a most dignified woman about my mother's age, in a simple yet elegant dress in bright spring colors. Her hair was fixed neatly in a bun, her head held high, heels clicking as she walked down the church steps. She smiled at me before heading down the path. I stopped and watched her walk away.

I'd never seen women like her before. Grace wore tight stretch pants and a dark form-fitting shirt. Her long, deep brown hair pulled back in a ponytail. Mom was far from poised, though you might see the occasional air of confidence once she'd gotten some whisky.

I went about my days and couldn't stop thinking about the little church. One day, after school, I walked through the front door.

"Are you open?" I asked a man at the front of the church, putting songbooks behind the pews.

He said, "We're *always* open. You're welcome to come in anytime."

"Thank you. I was hoping to come by on Sunday. What time does church start?"

He put down the books and headed towards me, offering a hand. "I'm Hank, the sole deacon—and handyman, Sunday school teacher, and a couple of other titles. We could use some younger patrons. What's your name?"

"Betty."

"Well, Betty, service starts at 10 a.m. I look forward to seeing you here."

I went that Sunday even though Debbie and Joyce are Catholic and teased me about it. My parents didn't discuss it, not even when I began going to church every Sunday.

Mom and Dad were atheists and didn't care about church...I did whatever I wanted, whether in church or playing the flute; they didn't encourage me either.

I loved going to church. I felt more at home with the people there, and I didn't have to do all that standing up and kneeling. They believed people should confess by talking to God and not to a guy in a booth. I knew I could trust God and never tell anyone else. I didn't have to wear fancy clothes and loved singing.

I was ready to experience new things. I was glad Mom and Dad didn't care what I did because I had no curfew, and no one told me no. I started hanging out at Bernice's Restaurant, where Debbie, Joyce, and I played pool in the back room. At the same time, Mom and Dad got drunk at Danny's Den or Kenny Carter's Kitten Club. Kenny Carter's had Go-Go dancers wearing miniskirts and white boots. We had antique car shows and carnivals at the ballpark. During Christmas, we had Santa Claus landing in a helicopter. We were a small town, but we were big time.

Chapter 10: Friends, Bullies, and Cheats

The summer of 1969 kept Americans on the edge of their seats. Neil Armstrong and Buzz Aldrin walked on the moon, and we were glued to our televisions as footage from outer space aired.

On August 15, Woodstock exploded onto the scene and was billed as "three days of Peace and Music." This would be a turning point for a nation of individuals who stood for peace, yet they rioted against the Government. The "Summer of Peace." would be a violent year.

Nixon brought our troops home from Vietnam, an event called "Vietnamization." Our troops, who risked their lives for freedom, were coming home from hell. It was sad that many of our young soldiers never returned home, and the ones who did were spat upon at the airport as soon as they stepped back onto American soil. Our men returned without homes, families, or limbs, surviving the best way they knew with no one to help them. If they didn't commit suicide, they begged on the streets or made a meager living out of vans, and some started taking drugs to numb the pain of violence they had experienced in Vietnam.

Many bogus news reports reported that our men were killing babies and raping innocent women over there, but only a few knew the truth. The North Vietnamese used children and women to get live grenades into American camps. They would strap bombs to them and make them walk to their deaths. Our government turned its backs on our men by refusing to acknowledge they had been exposed to cancer-causing agents such as Agent Orange. The people who sent these soldiers to mutilate the enemies of America are now watching these soldiers dying from the inside out.

I remember having many heated discussions with my dad over whether we should've ever gone to war in the first place. Of course, he was all for whatever the government decided to do. On the other hand, it was nothing more than a chess game of politics. Only our soldiers were the pawns they could sacrifice, and they were spilling their precious blood for their kings and queens in the government. I heard bits and pieces of what was happening like people spitting on them and riots everywhere.

In hindsight, my problems seem so trivial. I was thirteen and busy treading water in my private hell.

I had a lot of trouble breathing thanks to a deviated septum in my nose. The cartilage in my nose continuously moved to the right side for ten years. It felt like I could only breathe from the other nostril, which ruined my tonsils. The surgery happened just before the start of school to fix my deviated septum. I remember having two black eyes, and my whole head throbbed. I was dizzy for five days. The doctor had packed my entire sinus cavity with long strands of cotton. The doctor pulled the cotton from each nostril like a clown, removing the never-ending scarves from his sleeve. My sinuses were so dry and cracked that the pain made breathing difficult. I sneezed out scabs for four months. During the same time, I had to get my tonsils out just before the start of school in 1969. Breathing had become a painful chore once again. The doctor removed the bandages a few days before school started, revealing my swollen face on the first day.

I started the sixth grade in Mrs. Clifford's class, where I met a tall, red-haired girl named Roxanne. She had long, thin legs and a bigger chest than me, which meant the kids wouldn't be looking at just me. She was also from California, and she dressed nicely like me.

I liked her because she was older than her age, and I could relate to her. At first, she wasn't sure she wanted me as a friend because she knew I hung around with Debbie Barber and Joyce Brindamour. She thought they were the most "crude, rude, and obnoxious" people she'd ever met. Once she realized they were no reflection of who *I* chose to be, our friendship was sealed fast.

"So, why did you move here?"

"My Dad died a few years ago, and my mom met a guy who lives here. She packed me, my sister, and brother Lee, and moved us out here."

"You don't like it here?"

"No, I hate it. The kids are juvenile and dress ridiculously. Also, the girls are so childish."

"Not me. We dress alike. I love wearing nice clothes, but the other kids tease me."

"Do you go to church? What religion are you?"

"I'm Baptist; I joined the church on Narragansett Ave. It's nice, and I like the people."

"I'm a Pentecostal. I miss my church in California."

"Are those the people that jump around?"

"Yes, but it's called being in the spirit and talking in tongues."

"Do you believe all that stuff?"

"Yes, it helps me deal with my mother and her problems. She's always sick and takes a lot of pills. Sometimes, I don't know what to do for her. I need to escape, and the church does that for me."

"Wow, we have a lot in common. My parents both drink and the church helps me to escape. I sometimes go to Bernice's; you'll like it there."

As the months passed, we became good friends. Roxanne has always been a spiritual person, and like me, she had some tough times growing up. She and I bonded because we had fun and laughed while walking around town or at the seawall, away from the turmoil in our lives.

In the fall of 1969, Roxanne, Margaret, and I entered seventh grade. We could be loyal friends in school because their parents disapprove of me outside of school. I smoked, and, unfortunately, I was associated with the Barbers and Brindamours. The whole town knew that Mom and Dad were drunks, sometimes making it hard for me to make friends.

Having friends couldn't protect me from Martha, however. Martha had been abusing me for years. She found pleasure in knuckle-punching me in the arm. She left bruises on me so deep they didn't go away for weeks, meaning I often had bruises on top of them. When Martha felt particularly aggressive, she would rip my clothes and scratch me, then fling me around as she laughed at me. When she couldn't get my clothes, she grabbed my hair and pulled out bloody strands. Once, she punched me in my stomach with full force and left me gasping for air. By seventh grade, and at fourteen, I'd had enough.

She was not going to quit just because I ignored her. Someone wise once said, "If you do the same thing you've always done, you will get the same results." I couldn't be bullied for the rest of my school life, so I turned to the meanest girl I knew...Debbie Barber.

She was two grades higher than me, but everyone knew her reputation as one tough cookie. Everyone feared Debbie Barber, even Martha, because she won every fight. So, I asked her to teach me to stick up for myself.

Debbie and I worked in her yard daily for a week, during which time she taught me how to defend myself and block Martha's punches.

Debbie said, "They will always go after you if you look afraid. Be brave and act tough, and you'll be tough."

"I can't, Deb. She scares me. Fighting makes me shake, and I can't breathe. My whole body tightens up."

"Stop being a baby. Do you want Matha to beat your ass every yea until you graduate? Toughen up. Now, put youa arms up and protect youaself."

I spread my feet to stabilize myself and used my arms to brace against her attack, which worked. Deb hit me, but I protected myself.

"Okay, now you must learn how to kick her ass."

"No, I want to stop her from coming after me."

"She'll neva stop until you teach her a lesson. You'll have to beat her up."

"Is there any other way?"

"No, now stop and listen. Lean on youa front foot, but neva raise one of youa feet because you'll lose youa footing. When you swing at her, use all youa weight, not just youa arm."

"But what if she moves?"

"You have to anticipate where she will go. I've watched Matha beat up many kids; she usually moves to her right when she moves. Keep that in mind. Be quick and sure of youaself."

"I don't think I can ..."

"Stop whining, Betty, and let's try."

Securing my feet and leaning forward, I quickly drew back my fist and hit Deb in the jaw.

"Oh my God, Deb, I'm sorry. Oh, shit...I did it."

"Yep, that's ok. I didn't expect it from you, and neither will she. Youa ready."

This is my seventh grade, and Martha's reign of terror is over!

"Hey, Betty!" Martha yelled fifteen minutes before school. She was taunting me just enough to gather a crowd.

"Martha, you better leave me the hell alone. I'm warning you."

She pushed my shoulders, laughing, "What the hell will you do about it? You chicken shit!"

She pushed me again, and with my teeth clenched, I said, "Don't touch me!"

She laughed again and went to push me one more time. Before she could grab me, I grabbed her around her shirt, swung her around twice, and let her go. She went skidding in her skirt across the playground on her knees.

"Screaming at the top of her lungs, AAAAAhhhhh..."

Finally landing about seven feet away, she rolled over, crying and screaming. I felt terrible, but I couldn't let anyone see me cry. I glanced at her and saw the flesh ripped from her knees and hands, tiny pebbles, and sharp rocks embedded in the freshly torn skin. They saw her lying on the ground, clutching her knees and suffering in pain, and shocked everyone. There was silence as the teachers came out and took me inside when the ambulance arrived.

I was expelled from school immediately for fighting on school grounds. I went home and cried to my dad, knowing how disappointed he would be. When I told him what happened, he grabbed me by the hand and looked at me at eye level.

"Betty Lee, you stop that crying right now. I am proud of you for standing up to her like that. She got what she deserved. I wish you hadn't done it on school grounds. Now, let's take care of the idiots at your school."

We went to the school office, and Dad demanded to talk with the principal, Mr. McCarthy.

The secretary told Dad, "I'm sorry, Mr. Ott. He cannot be bothered right now. He is swamped."

That only made him angrier. "You go in there and tell that son of a bitch that I am here, and I need to see him now!"

"Mr. Ott, please." Dad was already headed to the door with the secretary calling after him. He slammed open the door and yelled at Principal McCarthy.

"What the hell do you mean expelling my daughter from school?" The principal got up slowly from his chair and calmly spoke.

"Mr. Ott, we don't allow fighting on school grounds. That is a rule that Betty is aware of. We had no choice."

"Then why didn't you do anything about that bully that bullied her daily in school? I never saw Martha Corr suspended for harassing all the other children."

"Well, technically, she didn't fight here on school grounds. It was just a little teasing here and there, normal kid stuff."

"There is nothing normal about tormenting children! My daughter has a right to go to school without getting harassed, and if you don't tell my daughter she can come back to school today, I will take you to court personally and sue you!"

"I am sorry, Mr. Ott. Please tell your daughter she is suspended but can't return for three days." Dad walked to the door and opened it. After talking to Mr. McCarthy, Dad and I went home.

Martha was up in traction for one week out of the two in the hospital. Even in her second week, she still picked out tiny rocks from her scarred knees. Martha's dad got angry when he found out I was only suspended. He was a five'5" small man with more bark than bite. He was at our door the day after Martha went to the hospital.

"Your daughter ruined Matha's knees. Her legs might have blood clots, and your daughter got away with no punishment! What are you gonna do about that?"

My Dad was angry, "Listen, you piece of shit, if you spent more time disciplining your daughter, she wouldn't have gotten what she deserved from mine. You let her bully my daughter and never did anything about it, so don't come up here trying to tell me how to raise my daughter. I am proud of Betty Lee for what she did. Your daughter learned a valuable lesson from her. Now get the hell away from my house!"

Dad slammed the door in his face and left him screaming.

"I'll sue you, Ott. I'll take everything you own for this!"

"Go ahead, Corr, and I will sue you right back for raising that monster!"

Mr. Corr never brought charges against us. Unfortunately, I would have to deal with Martha again to convince her it was over, but I was ready for her. With my Daddy behind me, I could do anything.

I was Daddy's little girl, but I was also Kurt's girlfriend in seventh grade. He was a tall, dark-haired Italian with a sexy bow-legged walk. We celebrated our birthdays together on April 6th, even though he was one year younger. He lived in Harbor Island, but we had fun working on his cars and playing records when we could get together. He was the first boy I allowed to touch me.

I still had a crush on my childhood sweetheart, Russell, in the seventh grade, but I knew we would never be more than just friends. He thought of me more like a little sister than anything else. His  Mom, Ginny, had a different opinion of our relationship. She had a dirty mind and accused us of having sex. She even got Roy to steal the $120 onyx ring I bought for Russell. I saved all summer to pay for that ring. She was vindictive. She told him to throw it into the ocean because our relationship was "dirty." I hated her for doing that. I didn't understand why she had to be so mean. Since *she* wasn't happy, she didn't want anyone else to be either.

I wrote all these little revelations about other people in my diary. That was the only place I could express my opinions and feelings where they mattered. I had to hide it on the garage's second floor since I caught Mom reading it. One day, when I went to the garage to write more of my secrets, Dad kept some of his own. As I rounded the corner, I saw Dad and Gail, the woman who lived across the street, lying naked on a mattress. I stopped dead in my tracks, then turned and ran down the steps. We never talked about it.

I knew Mom was cheating on Dad with her boss, Paul Talley, at the Co-op. I grew up knowing my parents were only together because it was convenient. Little did I know that their cheating and lack of love for each other would negatively influence my relationships for the rest of my life. My childhood was now in the past, only brought forward by memories.

Chapter 11: Identity Crises

Mom and Dad fit in perfectly with our neighbors, but I felt like a grape in a box of raisins. There was always a space within me that drove me to be curious about things. It wasn't long before I could control my curiosity about my real family. Were they more like me, driven to express and improve myself and not readily accept what life had given me? I wondered if I looked like my birth mother and if I had any siblings out there. I had no idea where my birth mother or father could be, so I tried to put them out of my mind.

In a way, I was grateful that Grace was not my natural mom. I didn't have to worry about inheriting the genes of alcoholic parents. At the same time, I wanted so much for them to notice me and be proud of me. No matter how hard I tried, I could never please mom.

I spent less time at home, and no one was there anyway. The summer before eighth grade, I had just turned fourteen, and Mom had taken on a job as a cook at Neptune on Ocean Road. I took that as my opportunity to eat some great Italian Subs for lunch occasionally. Sometimes, when she wanted fresh seafood, she would go to the Co-Op at Point Judith.

On one occasion, she took Ginny and two guys with us. They all got drunk at the Co-Op before we came home. I remember one of the Lobsters got loose in the car, and Mom went crazy. She almost wrecked the car, trying to get the thing back into the bag. We nearly ran right into the sea wall. It was horrifying to think that I was going to die.

It had been an entire school year since Martha tried to beat my ass, but now she had healed, and we lived within spitting distance, so it was a matter of time before she'd try again.

Joyce found a way to escape her mother as often as possible by coming to Narragansett for the summer. May was struck hard with Huntington's chorea, which affects the nervous system, causing fits of rage and uncontrollable jerky movements in the body. In addition, she struggled with bipolar disorder, which caused her unpredictable mood swings.

Joyce and I were sitting on an old wooden fence in the spacious backyard of a nearby neighbor's house, and Martha lived two houses down from there. We were there for 15 minutes when Martha showed up.

Walking toward us, she said, "The next time I see you in school, I'm gonna beat you so bad, no one will be able to recognize youa face," shaking her fist in my face.

As my stomach tightened and my heart started beating fast, I said, "Get away from me, Martha. I'm tired of all your crap. You don't intimidate me anymore. Just get the hell outta here and go home."

I stood tall next to the wooden western-style fence even though I wanted to run away. Martha got in my face and pushed me, but I grabbed her right arm and twirled her around, putting a choke hold on her. She tried to wiggle out of it. I grabbed the back of her head and spun her around so that her neck was pushed up against the fence with my forearm putting pressure on the front and back of her neck. She started to turn purple as Joyce screamed, "Betty! Stop it! Get off her; you're gonna kill her! BETTY LEE!!!"

I let go of her when she became limp, and she fell at my feet. My body shook, and my legs felt like jelly from the adrenaline.

"Don't ever come near me again," I said, gritting my teeth and walking away from her.

And she never did.

Soon after, I enrolled in the Barbizon Modeling School in Providence. Dad spared no expense to take me to the four-month-long training course that would transform me into a lady. The path to beauty was long and arduous.

First, my smile would have to be fixed. I didn't smile much because of the Lauren Hutton gap between my front teeth. I also didn't get two of my second teeth in the front or my wisdom teeth, so Dad told the dentist to pull the five teeth in front and give me a partial plate. It was cheaper and quicker than having braces for two years. I remember thinking I should've been allowed to keep my teeth at fourteen years old. It was cruel to have them yanked out because they didn't want to deal with the hassle and expense of braces.

Other things changed as well. I traded my blue jeans and psychedelic tops for fancy dresses; Roxanne was delighted to make my gowns for the runway.

I started taking better care of my nails and traded my ponytail for long, straight hair. I learned to walk like a lady while spending hours on the runway. After painfully plucking my Brook Shields eyebrows until they were red and swollen, I was taught to use makeup to accentuate my best features. It astonished me to see what some girls sacrificed to impress people.

The real sacrifice was losing my status as Daddy's Little Girl. Dad felt that to make me a true lady, he would have to take away my childhood toys. He stopped taking me to the stock car races and started taking Jimmy and Roy. All the familiar things I had come to love from childhood were quickly snatched away.

I was disappointed with the adults in my life. I became increasingly rebellious because of what I was forced to go through physically, coupled with the lack of care from my alcoholic stand-ins. Mom and Dad never tried to talk to me about my depression. Whatever bond we had between us was ripped away, leaving only memories.

Dad found more reasons to be disappointed in me as time went on. My metamorphosis from tomboy to lady attracted some older guys. Kurt, my first childhood boyfriend from 6th grade, was a year younger than me. He offered me no solace when I needed him, so I looked elsewhere.

Dad was not too happy with my new change. I didn't care because he didn't spend enough time with me for his opinion to matter. I strived to make somebody happy with me because I needed to feel affirmation from someone. Anyone at all would do. What did I do to make someone notice I was alive?

Margaret, Roxanne, and I spent more time together in the hall at school, but their parents still didn't want them to be around me. Although Mom wanted me to fit in with Joyce and Debbie, I knew inside that I only felt sorry for Joyce and feared Debbie.

Debbie and her mother, Ginny, tried to get between Margaret and me, but to their dismay, Margaret remained a loyal friend, at least in school. Ginny, Debbie, and Roy did everything they could to make my life miserable. Debbie threatened me, and they threw eggs at our car and house on Halloween. This was the end of my relationship with Debbie.

Joyce and Debbie always thought I had a perfect life. The spoiled brat who got everything she wanted. They couldn't see behind closed doors, and I couldn't tell anyone about the drinking and the fighting. The truth was that my parents were paying me to keep quiet. The record player, recorder, beautiful bedroom set, bike, and dolls were distractions, so they didn't have to spend time with me. I got new ice skates because they had a knockdown, drag-out fight.

My friends never suspected alcoholism and neglect; they never knew the private hell that was my home life. I was forbidden to discuss family business with anyone because Mom and Dad didn't want me to embarrass them.

Grace had a knack for getting under my skin, even all these years later. If only she'd told me about my birth mother sooner.

In the summer of 1971, a handful of 15-year-olds at my school and I attended Driver's Education. I was the only one who couldn't produce a birth certificate or, in my case, adoption papers.

Since it was at my teacher's request, Mom couldn't avoid my questions about my birth. I caught her one afternoon in the kitchen; fortunately, she was sober.

"Mom, where are my birth certificate and adoption papers?"

"Why on earth would you need them?"

"The Driver's Ed teacher said we needed birth certificates to get our permits and Social Security cards."

"Why can't you just use your Navy identification?"

"Mom, she said we *had* to have the certificates. The ID card won't work for this."

"I'm sure we can figure something out."

"Why can't you just find my birth certificate?"

Sighing, Mom sat at the table, pulled out a Raleigh, and lit it. She said, "Betty Lee, you are asking me to find something from a long time ago. I haven't the slightest clue where it would be."

"Please, mom. I can't get a permit or a job without it! Would Dad know where the papers are?"

"No—he wouldn't know anything about that stuff."

"Mom, we need to find them—"

"Betty! Just stop. Listen for a second and stop nagging me." Mom looked down at the table and mumbled, "We never sent for it."

"What? I couldn't hear you."

"We never sent for it, Betty."

"But why not? I don't understand. Why wouldn't you get it? Didn't you have to have one to adopt me?" Mom looked up at me and said nothing.

"Well then, how about my adoption papers? I'm sure they'll accept those." The silence was louder than any voice I had heard.

"Mom...You did adopt me...right? I mean, that's what you told me all these years."

"Betty, try to understand. It was a tough time back then. Your dad's blood pressure was high, and he didn't want to go through the physical for the adoption for fear that we would lose you. Your mother wanted your birth to be kept quiet. We didn't want to draw any attention."

"So...you didn't adopt me then?"

"No, we didn't," she said, stubbing out her cigarette. "Your mother is my niece. She...."

"So then, I'm not an Ott. I don't even know what my real name is! What *is* my name? Who do I belong to, Mom?" I was right in her face.

"Your name is Ott. That is what you've always gone by."

"What's my *real* name?"

"It's Elizabeth Lee DuPass."

"DuPass…That's just great, Mom."

With nothing left to say, I stormed out, hurt and disgusted. My whole life had been a lie. In my room, I threw myself onto my bed. *I wasn't even adopted; what the hell kind of mother would leave her newborn on the doorstep of alcoholics instead of a legally vetted adoption?*

The more I thought about it, the angrier I got. *I knew Mom was a liar, but I didn't think she would lie about something this big. What other secrets were kept from me?* I went back into the kitchen.

"I still need those documents. Why did you lie to me all those years? You know what, I don't want to know."

And all I could think was, what was wrong with me that my mother had to get rid of me? Why did she have to keep my birth a secret? Why didn't Bob and Grace adopt me?

"You're being dramatic, Betty. No one got rid of you. Mary had no choice; she had to give you up, or she would lose her other two children. It was a tough decision. And Betty, we loved you like you were our own. How could you be so ungrateful after everything we've done for you? A piece of paper is not going to make a difference."

"Ungrateful? How could you—you don't get it…It's about my identity…*then it hit me. It was pointless. To mom, I was being a whiny baby, an ungrateful kid. She didn't get it. She'd lived in an orphanage. By her standards,*

112

I was lucky to have her and her dad. I was wasting my breath. Still, I needed my birth certificate.

"Mom, that piece of paper is important to me. What do we need to do to get it?"

"I'll take care of your birth certificate. Just give me time; now, go away."

In the meantime, I convinced my teacher that Mom had to send away the documents and that it would be a couple of weeks.

From this point on...I realized that my life as I knew it was a lie. The truth altered my attitude toward everything; it all seemed so pointless.

With no curfew, every weekend was a new chance to see what else I could experience. We would sit on big blankets, smoking pot and drinking Boone's Farm Apple Wine at the concerts. We stayed "Toasted and Roasted" on breezy summer evenings. The cops would walk by the blankets and not say anything because they would have to arrest everyone at the concert if they did. I loved it because I was more of a flower child than a Hippie amid freedom at its peak.

Mom and Dad lived their pathetic lives, and I lived mine. I may have owed them for not abandoning me, but my respect for them was waning.

Chapter 12: Raped by Society

As I sat in the Airport waiting to board my flight, I scanned the waiting area, watching everyone go by and see how different they were. Less than eight years ago, people from other ethnic backgrounds were prohibited from eating or sitting in certain places with whites. I remember watching the riots on TV in 1971.

Nixon had just enforced desegregation.

Opposing races of people struggled to keep their heritage despite the forced assimilation of their people. They had to figure out who they were in this changing culture and what they would fight for to gain equality. Amid all the shootings, beatings, burning crosses, and looting, people protested in the street to fight for their place in society.

At the same time, I found myself walking mindlessly to find an identity that was kept from me. I always felt deep inside that I didn't belong in my surroundings; on the other hand, Joyce seemed content in her world, never longing for anything different. She lived in the city and hung out with new friends. She found another best friend, Millie, who lulled her into the pacifying world of marijuana and cocaine. She quickly discovered that this was much more convenient than facing stress in the real world.

There was something about Millie I didn't like. Joyce thought I was jealous, but I was disgusted by the wrinkled, dirty clothes draped from her anorexic frame and messy, dull, brown hair. Her face was blotched with uneven skin, and her teeth were brown. Millie had lost an eye as a child, which I imagine is why Joyce took to her. Being with someone with a disability helped Joyce feel better about her situation.

114

Debbie started hanging around with new friends who introduced her to multiple sex partners and the slew of diseases that went with it. She had successfully ostracized herself from the white community. Roxanne spent all her free time at her church and had a different class of friends. I was happy for her, but at the same time, I felt alone when she was away. I was running away from my past as fast as possible; however, I had nowhere to go without any destination. I was not born in Rhode Island, nor did I have siblings like the rest of my friends. At that moment, I'd been in Narragansett for nine years and still didn't know who I was, not just by name but emotionally. I knew I wouldn't find it at home, so I spent my weekends away as much as possible.

If mom refused to drop me off in the city at Joyce's, I would hitchhike there on the weekends. Traveling on the highways was fun. Anyone could hitch in VW Beetles and Chevy vans painted with flower power and peace signs in vibrant yellows and purples. It was groovy to see vans with full-sized beds in the back.

Joyce and I took advantage of the concerts that came to Brown University. The students there were still protesting the Vietnam War. Longhaired hippies adorned with goatees in fur vests, saying, "Peace, man!" Although the colors and styles made everyone *seem* happy and peaceful, a fire raged within every man and woman to rise against "The Man."

In contrast to the KKK, the Black Panther Party was formed to fight for the African American community's rights and individualism, which the establishment continued to deny. Many older people, including my parents, were not ready to accept that they were equal to everyone else.

No one trusted President Nixon, affectionately known as Tricky Dicky, who was serving his first presidential term. He would be impeached before the end of his second term. The time of free sex didn't mean the same to everyone. Some would take what they wanted despite another's objections, and I was forced into an event that would change my life forever. It was a Friday night in September of 1971 when it happened. It was the perfect night for a crime if my life were a horror movie cliché. There were no lights on Brown Street. A new moon was out, and the darkness loomed with a thickness that could swallow you whole. I could hear the leaves skittering across the streets as the wind howled and branches raked against the side of the house. I was fifteen years old. Dad was working the graveyard shift at the Peace Dale Processing Mill. He always left the house around 10 p.m. to stop at Bess Eaton Donuts in Wakefield for a bite and coffee before work. Mom feverishly rushed around the house to prepare with May and Ginny for the bar. She always got ready after Dad left because she didn't want him to know she was going out at night, but he knew.

The windows were all closed, but they had so much paint on them they wouldn't lock. I had no plans except to sit around in mom's rocker in the living room in my PJs and watch old movies on TV until I fell asleep. I woke up around one a.m. Mom wasn't home yet, so I left the door unlocked for her and went to bed. I knew she'd be angry if I made her look for her keys because she couldn't open the door after drinking.

I was so exhausted that I don't remember falling asleep.

Suddenly, shocked into consciousness, I awoke to find a hand across my mouth. I looked to see Brian, the twenty-three-year-old man who lived upstairs, hovering over me.

"Take off your clothes, and don't make a sound," he said through clenched teeth.

I could smell whiskey on his breath as he spoke. I hated that smell. I'd spent my entire life smelling whiskey on mom's breath, and smelling it again invoked my anger. I lashed out at Brian. He was drunk and stupid and wouldn't take advantage of me. Who did he think he was, coming into my house like that?

I forced his hand away from my mouth and told him, "Get out, or I'll scream. Get out!"

Just then, I heard a noise in the living room. It was Mom coming home. She slammed the door open, making a loud noise as it hit the sewing machine. He leaned down over me and said, "If you say anything about this, I'll come back some night and kill you." Brian lifted my bedroom window and jumped out. I could feel the adrenalin surging through my veins as I got out of bed on shaky legs to ensure Mom was home.

In a sharp tone, slurring her words, Mom said, "Why are you still up? Go to bed."

She didn't notice anything was wrong, and I didn't say anything because I believed Brian would surely kill me if I told anyone. It was no secret that he beat his wife and kids when he got drunk. It was common for his wife, Cindy, to emerge from the apartment with black eyes and bruises up and down her arms. Screams and sobbing could be heard from his boys as they got their weekly beatings.

I didn't tell Mom for many reasons. However, it was mostly because she was drunk. Also, she would not be able to process what happened. I locked the front door, put on my blue jeans and a T-shirt, and stayed in my room with the light on. Fear kept me from walking around the house because he would hear me and come back. He and his wife were upstairs fighting again. Eventually, I must have fallen asleep because I woke up when I heard Dad coming in around 8 a.m. It was unusual that he would come home early instead of going to the bar until noon, but then I remembered he was going out tonight and needed rest. I wished I could tell him what had happened the night before, but I feared Brian.

I was still worried about what happened and wanted to tell my parents, but they never took anything I said seriously. Dad had such a bad temper; he would either blame me or kill Brian, so I did nothing.

The next day was Saturday; typically, at 15, I would be outside at the beach or hanging out with my friends.

But I couldn't bring myself to walk out of the front door. I felt this invisible force field of fear around the apartment, so I stayed home all day watching TV and listening to music. I feared leaving because Brian was up and down the stairs all day. I didn't want to see him, but more than that, I didn't want *him* to see me.

That night, Mom and Ginny were planning to go out again. I overheard their conversation on the phone and started to panic. My heart started to race. What was I going to do if Brian came back? Since Dad was off, he was headed to the bar, too. I didn't want to be alone.

As Mom started to get ready, I felt a panic attack and asked her to please stay home with me because I didn't feel good.

"What are you talking about? How come you didn't mention this before?"

"I felt fine before."

"I'm going out, don't be silly. You're not a baby," she said, dismissing me.

"Can I go to Debbie's house and spend the night then? I'll be home early in the morning to do my chores."

Mom got on the phone with Ginny and asked, "Can Betty spend the night over there with Debbie." I overheard Ginny say, "No, I don't want her here with Roy in the house with no adult around. I don't trust them."

Ginny had such a dirty mind all the time. She succeeded in breaking up the friendship between Russell and me, and now she thought I wanted Roy! Ughh! His very presence made me ill.

Mom hung up the phone. "Just go to bed if you don't feel good and try to do those dishes and sweep up here. I'll be home later."

Eventually, I went to my room, having convinced myself I was being irrational. Brian wouldn't try anything again so soon.

When I heard the front door close as Mom left for the night, I ran to lock the door and checked the whole house to ensure all the windows were shut tight, securing those that could be closed. I got a big knife from the kitchen and sat in the living room watching TV. If he did try to get in, I would hear him. I listened quietly to all the footsteps upstairs while I waited for Mom and Dad to come home.

Dad staggered in around 1:30 a.m., went directly to his bedroom, right next to mine, and shut the door. I changed into my nightgown and sat on the edge of my bed, waiting to hear Mom come home. I didn't want her to see me up this late again. About forty-five minutes after Dad came home, I heard the front door slam shut and a thump on the other side of my bedroom wall in the kitchen as Mom fell into her chair at the table. She always fell asleep in that chair, but lately, she'd been falling onto the floor, so I got up and put her to bed.

She swung her arm at me, saying, "Leave me alone and go to bed."

I was so exhausted from worrying and waiting that I locked the door, returned to my room, and passed out.

After a week passed, I figured he wouldn't come back. Brian wasn't used to women who fought back. I kept my secret and prayed that I was right.

It didn't seem like I was asleep for long when a cold chill shivered through my body while I was sleeping. I searched for my blankets without opening my eyes but realized I couldn't find them. I reluctantly opened my eyes to see Brian standing over me again. I breathed to scream, but he pressed his cold sweaty hand down on my mouth and said, "If you make a sound, I'll slit your throat." He raised a long, thin filet knife to my face to ensure I would see it. The blade glimmered from the reflection of the light outside my window. I started whimpering through his hand because I knew how violent he was and thought he would kill me. I tried to be quiet but couldn't stop crying and shaking. He kept telling me, "Shut up, or I'll kill you." He climbed up on my bed, putting his knees on the outside of my legs. I resisted as much as possible by trying to keep my body rigid while he pressed the knife harder against my throat. I tried to push his chest away, but he grabbed my hands and held them together over my head, squeezing them hard against the headboard.

He briefly laid the knife on my chest to tear off my underwear. Quickly picking up the knife, he pressed it hard against my throat.

Whimpering, I said, "No, please, no, no, please."

"Shut up, or I'll kill you now!" Brian said in a loud whisper through his clenched teeth.

His face was red from struggling with me. Bulging eyes glared at me in hatred while his putrid breath made condensation on my face. His weight was on me now, and it was hard to breathe. My words seemed to run together as I begged him not to continue. He forced his knees between my legs one last time and penetrated my body. I felt him tearing into me, and pain surged through my abdomen and legs as he pushed harder. I tried to disappear and become numb. I told myself repeatedly, *this isn't happening.* He may have taken my body, but he wouldn't have the satisfaction of subjecting my mind to him. Thank God it was over quickly. The knife was still against my throat when he ejaculated in me. He let go of my hands and got up. I rolled over and curled up on my side.

"You say anything about this or tell anyone, and I will come back and kill you." He walked out the front door past Mom.

I tried to scream and move, but I couldn't. Nothing would come out. It felt like he was still sitting on my chest, and I couldn't breathe. I had no air. Suddenly, I heard a scream and realized it was me. It was a blood-curdling scream that went on until there was no more breath in me. I didn't notice Dad shaking me. I pushed him away and grabbed my blanket to cover up. I knew he was speaking to me, but I couldn't make out his words. All I could do was cry hysterically. He must have thought I was having a nightmare because he again grasped my shoulders and yelled at me to wake up.

"Betty Lee, wake up. Are you all right?"

I screamed again and managed to force out the words, "Brian raped me; he had a filet knife and said he would kill me if I said anything."

"What?"

I told him again.

"Get dressed," he said. He went into his room and put his pants on.

I couldn't bring myself to move. Dad came back into my room.

"Get dressed right now," he said in a demanding voice.

He woke Mom at the table and told her, "Call the police and tell them Brian just came into our house and raped Betty."

Mom said, "What? What's going on?"

Dad said, "Just do it. I'm going upstairs to find out what the hell happened here." I heard Dad slam the front door and run up the stairs.

Mom called the police and said, "You better get up before Bob kills Brian. He just raped Betty Lee."

Mom hung up the phone and came into my room with a weird look on her face. "How the hell did he get in?"

Sensing her implication, I looked up at her in disgust. She glared at my tear-stained face, "Did you lock the front door after you came home?"

I heard her breath catch. "WELL, DID YOU?" I said, yelling at her through my sobs.

I could hear Dad screaming through their front door upstairs, "Unlock this fucking door now. Open the door, or I'll break it down." I heard Dad banging with his fist, trying to knock the door down.

Brian and Cindy yelled at Dad to go away, saying, "What the hell do you want?"

I heard the door slam against the wall, and Dad started screaming at Brian, "What were you doing in my daughter's bedroom? Did you rape her? Where's the knife? Where is the knife, Brian? WHAT DID

YOU DO WITH IT?" Dad said, frantically turning over drawers in the kitchen.

I heard their silverware hit the floor and Dad's heavy feet above my head, searching through the house.

Brian said, "What knife? Are you crazy?"

Cindy looked bewildered, "What's going on, Brian? What did you do?"

Mom was standing on the stairs, halfway between our two apartments, so she could hear what they were saying.

She looked down at me and said, "What have you done?" "I didn't do anything! He came down into my room while you and Dad passed out! It's not my fault!"

I didn't want Dad to go to prison, so I stayed close, sobbing and crying, hugging my arms tight around my shivering body. I still had Brian's smell all over me.

Dad peered at Brian while telling Cindy, "He raped Betty Lee at the point of a filet knife." Her eyes darted over to him. She walked over to Brian until she was close to his face and asked, "What did you do? Where is the knife?"

Cindy scrambled to find the knife among the silverware on the floor, but it wasn't there.

The Chief of Police and one other officer responded. They moved past Mom and me on the stairwell to the yelling coming from inside. Dad had already been searching the house for the evidence. Just before the police entered, Dad found the knife in the bathroom's bottom laundry basket. The police immediately started questioning Brian as he was put in handcuffs and taken to jail.

The police took me to the South County Hospital, where I had an internal physical. The doctor noted bruising on my upper thighs, the fronts of my legs, my wrists, and inside my vaginal area. The conclusion was rape while being restrained. I struggled to recount the rape through choking sobs and tears. I was humiliated. The doctor wrapped up his notes, and the police left the room to give me privacy.

Mom peered up at the ceiling. "I can't believe this is happening."

"Oh, shut up, Grace, we're going." Dad looked over at me and, as he put his arm around me, said, "Come on, honey, you need to rest. Let's go home."

For the next two days, I did nothing but curl up in bed and sob. I told my friends I was sick and couldn't go out. The police escorted Brian to get his things, and he was forced to stay with his mother in Wakefield until the trial. The judge put a restraining order against him so he couldn't be in the same city as me. It was a nice gesture, but it didn't make me feel any better about what had happened to me.

Mom and Dad pressed charges against Brian. Unfortunately, they didn't have as much money as Brian's family. They couldn't afford an excellent lawyer to follow the whole ordeal through to the end. We lived in such a small town that everyone drew their conclusions about what happened that night. The most popular rumor was that I always invited Brian into my bedroom, but I charged him with rape to get back at him when he wouldn't leave his wife.

Dad was so humiliated and angry that he didn't talk to me for weeks. I don't think he knew what to say. When we went to court, he sat quietly in the hall. The judge ordered Brian and his family to move out of Narragansett for good so he couldn't bother me again. While he and his wife got their belongings, the police told me to leave town for two days. I felt like *I* was the one being punished for the heinous crime *he* committed. It wasn't fair; was this justice?

I missed my periods during the court proceedings for those three months. Mom said it was because of all the stress and that I would be fine, but I wasn't. Dad stayed out and drank every day after work. I felt I had disappointed him. His reaction made me feel ten times worse. He lashed out at me one day for wearing shorts and tank tops, saying, "If you wore more clothes around town, this never would've happened." I felt ashamed and dirty. I tried to scrub away the rape, leaving my skin raw in hot water. I couldn't get Brian's smell off me, and the nasty feeling didn't go away, no matter how many showers I took.

Thinking about my ordeal fifteen years later still brings tears to my eyes. I can't breathe with this lump in my throat. Glancing up from my seat in the airport, I noticed a young teenage girl looking at me and wondering if she, too, had gone through anything horrendous. Silently to myself, I say a little prayer. "God, I hope not."

His smell wasn't all that he left with me that night. Though I thought the worst was over, I was about to learn that my nightmare was only beginning. I was pregnant. Mom knew it before I did, and she quickly planned to have the baby "removed" in the city.

I was scared to death to go through the procedure. The doctors kept telling me I wouldn't feel a thing and that this was done all the time. Despite their reassurance, I didn't feel any better. I was cold and shivering. Tears stung my eyes, and I couldn't stop crying. I got little sympathy from Mom and Dad. They just stared at me, the disappointment evident in their eyes. *"If you wore more clothes around town, this never would've happened."* I felt like everything was my fault. I hated my life.

I tensed up as they put me on the cold table and positioned my feet in the stirrups. I tried to look around at all the equipment in the room and the activity around me. I could hear the doctors and nurses talking about me as if I weren't there. I began shivering more violently. The more I tried to calm down, the more I shook. I thought they would sedate me, but they gave me a local, so I was awake for the whole procedure. I heard a loud vacuum noise. A few minutes later, I felt pain sear through my abdomen as the doctor inserted a cold instrument inside and into my cervix. I grabbed the sides of the unyielding steel table and tensed up as I cried out. Then, they scraped the inside of my uterus to clean out the pregnancy. They took twenty minutes to extract the remnants of my inner strength and Brian. I should have felt relieved. Instead, I was overcome with sadness. They killed my baby. It made me think about how fragile life is, and I would never do this again.

I was cramping more than I had ever felt during my worst period. I held my stomach and drew myself up into the sheet.

Another nurse came in. "Roll over; we have to give you a shot."

"What's it for?" I asked.

"It's called a RhoGAM shot. You have A-negative blood, which means your blood cells will attack any future foreign objects that are in your body. The shot will keep your body from rejecting any future pregnancies."

My stomach churned, and I wanted to throw up all over her shoes. The room was spinning. I rolled on my side as she plunged the needle into my backside. When she finished, someone else told me I could put my clothes back on and go.

It was the second most challenging thing I had ever been forced to do. I couldn't stop thinking about it on the long trip home. Was the baby a girl or a boy? Did God have plans for this child? Why did I feel so much guilt about it? Was the pain I felt my punishment for getting rid of the baby? The doctors allowed me to feel the immense pain as a lesson to not getting pregnant again. I wondered if they even knew or cared about the rape.

I rationalized it in my head over and over that the baby was from a rape. I hated Brian. Why would I want to look at this child daily and see its face? My feelings of anger would be taken out on my child. I was too young, hadn't finished school, and had no way of feeding a baby. No, this was the best thing to do, and I needed to forget about it and go on. I wiped the tears from my face and tried to be strong. I would tell no one this; not even he knew why I was in such pain. I told her I had the worst period I've ever had. I didn't want to give Ginny confirmation that what she had always said about me was true, either. She and others thought little of me all my life, and I had no confidence to rise against them. They were adults, but I held contempt and hatred for them for spreading all those vicious lies.

I couldn't go anywhere in town without feeling everyone whispering behind me. Every time I turned around, I saw Brian's face. *"If you say anything to anyone, I'll come back and kill you."* I saw him driving around by the pier a few times. There he was, banned from the town of Narragansett, yet I still had to fear him. I always cried, thinking about how rotten my life had become. When I wasn't crying, I was on the verge of tears. I didn't want to leave my room, and I didn't want to go back to school. This was the beginning of many years of therapy so that I could try to normalize. Mom and Dad were arguing more than ever about whether they were drunk that night.

Kurt, the one person I always thought I could turn to, could not face the reality of what had happened to me. He didn't know how to process the inundation of rumors constantly surrounding me. He was at a loss for words and found himself unable to approach me, and this was the one time in my life I needed him to hold me and tell me everything would be okay.

I did all I could to avoid facing my existence, which seemed worse because of the injustice in the town of Narragansett.

The Narragansett Police Department charged Brian on September 16, 1972, with rape, breaking, and entering (B & E), intending to commit rape. By October, the Washington County Courts and his attorney reduced the charges to Assault and B & E. His punishment for taking away my self-respect, dignity, and life, as I knew it, was one year in the Adult Correctional Institute and one year of probation. Still, the court suspended the sentence and only gave him one year probation. They brought up my past and tried to use the fact that I had an older boyfriend against me.

In November 1972, while still on probation, he was charged with Assault with a deadly weapon (a cue stick) and found guilty, yet Brian never spent one day in jail. By the end of 1974, Brian's record had been completely erased from the court archives. He was no longer considered a sexual predator of minors. I couldn't believe that they decided that I wasn't worth the justice that Brian deserved. It took him ten minutes to take my dignity away and less than a year to be exonerated. Getting through it would take me the better part of my life.

Chapter 13: Daughter Delayed

Love and peace ruled, and sex was carefree. We were living in the era of "free love" when self-preservation, drugs, sex, and alcohol marked the sign of the times, and I fell right into them. I needed to be wanted by someone, so I stayed out late, met new people, and flirted with many guys. I enjoyed the parties, the pot, and especially the attention of men. I will find out later. Unfortunately, my birth mother's need for companionship fell to me like a bad apple.

Although I was saturating myself with new experiences every day, one thing remained the same…my unresolved feelings about my beginnings. I wondered if my birth mother went through the same things I did when she was a kid. Did I look like her? Did she have problems with her teeth and sinuses, too?

I decided to ask Mom about my biological grandmother, her sister. If I could contact her, I could get to my birth mom.

I approached Mom, sitting in her favorite chair in the kitchen, under the old black rotary phone in the corner.

In a calm voice, I said, "Mom, can I ask you about my grandmother?"

"Sure, what do you want to know, sweetie?" As she smiles up at me.

"Do you have any idea where my grandparents are living?"

"Well, I send a Christmas card to my sister Myrtle every year, but they always come back unopened with the words, *return to sender*. She gets them but prefers not to answer."

Hmmm. Christmas Cards.

I asked, "Is it okay to search through the Christmas stuff to see the address you sent the card to?"

"No, that's fine. What are you going to do when you find the address?"

"I wanted to contact my birth Grandmother to see if she can give me Mary's Address."

"Are you sure you want to find her? She may not want to be found. She may be married with kids by now, and you might upset her entire life. Are you ready to be disappointed again?"

My throat felt like it was closing, and I couldn't breathe as I hesitated to say, "I don't know, I didn't think about that. What should I do?"

"You're almost sixteen, and your father and I knew this day would come soon, but I'm not ready. We love you, and we don't want you to leave."

As those words left her bright red lips, I couldn't believe my mother was saying something so sweet. I wanted to hug her, but she wasn't into that. I didn't know what to say, so after thanking Mom, I started my journey into the unknown.

Rummaging through the living room closet, I found the box behind a box full of old 33 and 45 records. Unopened Christmas cards were addressed to my Grandmother Myrtle in Albuquerque,

New Mexico. I snatched the letters and ran to my room, eager to contact her. I began to write these words…

Hello Grandmother,

My name is Betty Lee Ott. I was born Betty Lee DuPass, and my mother's name is Mary. When I was three days old, I was left with your sister Grace and her husband Bob Ott. They took me from the hospital. My mother, Mary, left San Diego after I was born and went to Chicago, but I don't know where she lives now.

I need to contact her. I want to talk to her to get to know her and more about myself. I've never had a grandmother.

I don't know if you know about me, but I want to learn everything about my real family. Do I have any siblings? Do I have any uncles or cousins? I am 16 now and can take care of myself. I don't need anyone to care for me anymore. That's why I'm trying to find my mother. I'm curious about why I have medical problems and want to see if I look like my mother.

Please don't be angry with me or mad at Mary. I don't want to cause any problems for anyone with this letter. I don't know how else to find my mother. Can you write back to me or call me? My phone number is 401-783-5555. My address is 26 Brown St., Narragansett, RI. 02882. Please get in touch with me; I'm home by 3:30 every day from school.

Sincerely, Betty Lee

I have held the letter for about a month and wondered if I should send it. If I didn't, I'd never know…If I did, I may never get an answer and anger many people. My mother was trying to find me, or she never wanted to hear from me. It was a tough and heartbreaking choice to make.

I finally sent the letter and a picture to Albuquerque, NM, with no return address on the outside because Myrtle always returned Grace's cards. I never told her about being raped by my neighbor and thinking about it now was why I had to go anywhere away from here.

Two weeks later, I received a letter from my natural mother, postmarked in Algonquin, IL. As I turned the letter repeatedly, my thoughts ran wild. Was I ready to meet my mother? I ripped it open and started to read:

Dear Betty Lee,

My mother contacted me almost immediately after receiving your letter. She was shocked to hear that I had a child she knew nothing about, as it would've made it difficult for me to keep you at the time. I had a difficult choice to make. I could keep you and give up my life in Chicago and lose the two children I'd already come to love or give you up to Grace and Bob. They had no children and loved you very much.

Only later, when you were about five years old, did I learn how you were treated. I tried to find you in San Diego, but your parents had already taken you and left. I remarried and had two more children. My third husband and I are raising five kids. Kenny and Kathy are older than you, Keith and Kyle are from my second marriage, and Katelyn is our youngest. We have a lovely house in Algonquin, IL. Kenny just entered the Marines and will get married soon, and Kathy works at the bank.

I know what it's like to be curious; I've been curious about your appearance and how you will turn out for years. Please believe me when I tried to find you; I wanted to raise you with my second husband. I told him and my two oldest all about you, and we would bring you home. Grace and Bob didn't adopt you, so I knew I could get you, but you had gone.

The three youngest children know nothing about my indiscretions. I haven't said anything to them about you because I never thought I would get to see you again. I want to meet you and find out what kind of young lady you turned out to be, but for right now, until I tell my family about you, I would prefer we only write. I hope you understand that this is a very delicate subject to bring up after all these years. My mother has made it clear that she never wants to talk to me again after deceiving them as I did. Your letter has caused a giant rift in my relationship with my parents. I'll have to live with that, but I think it best we only write for now.

It wouldn't be right to meet at this time. We shouldn't see each other until you turn eighteen and can make legal decisions. It would just complicate my life more and cause Grace and Bob pain. I hope you understand my position and reasons for this decision and that you will continue to write to me. Please forgive me; I never meant for any of this to turn out this way.

Sincerely, Mary

The last words of the letter left me feeling cold and empty. I was in tears. It was like I applied for a job and was rejected: *Sorry, Betty, the position of long-lost daughter does not need to be filled at this time.* I wasn't good enough to be adopted by the Ott's, and now I wasn't good enough to be a part of my *real* family. I was akin to dirt they swept under the rug and hid from the rest of the world. My court-appointed psychiatrist increased my sessions to two times a week.

It has been said that the father's sins will be revisited on the son. What about the sins of the mother? Although I never knew my mother, I began to recognize myself in her from the letters and phone calls we had made over the next two years. As she revealed bits and pieces of herself and the events that led to my birth, I realized she didn't know as much about my father as she led me to believe. Every time we touched on the subject, his name would change from Stevens to Stuart to Stewart, and the circumstances surrounding my conception and how they met would be different each time. I wasn't getting anywhere with her to discover who I was. My frustration would only lead me to ask more questions.

My birth certificate arrived after I turned fifteen, and I am officially a DuPass. *Betty Lee DuPass, who* is she? My new name was foreign as if someone had just picked it from a phonebook and slapped it on me. Before I could get my Social Security card, we had to go to court and legally change my name to Ott. In hindsight, I realized this name change would keep the Ott's out of trouble more than it would help me. If anyone knew they took me across state lines without being legal, someone would have done some jail time. The Ott name never made me proud, but at least it was familiar, and I *struggled* to be a part of something familiar. My birth certificate would bring me no closure.

I sent my Social Security card with my name change documents while I got my driver's permit. Mom was only happy that I got a license because she lost hers again. She saw it as a way for me to taxi her around in the car.

I started working at Burger Chef in Wakefield under my new name. It was 1972, and I had my first job. I was on my way to legal freedom from my parents. Unfortunately, I didn't get along with one of the girls who worked there, and I quit my first *real* job a few months later.

I had just graduated from the ninth grade, but with no high school in our town, I had to choose one of the three high schools I would attend. I'd been deserted by childhood friends who resented me for not accepting the road well-traveled and lost without a roadmap. I couldn't give up; I knew something else was out there, and I would never find it by staying here.

Part 3: Rambling

Chapter 14: Shrinking My Demons

In the Spring of 1972, Kurt and I were officially over, but it took a few years to get over him. I met Bobby Calgaricci at my lowest point while visiting with Joyce in the city. He was twenty and had an over-the-road job from Maine to Florida.

I found my independence in his free spirit. Bobby helped me realize I had to let go of Kurt, even though I loved him and thought of him often. Bobby helped distract me from the pain I was trying to escape, but inside, it was still eating like a tapeworm disease, slowly killing me.

During the most frightening times, I withdrew into myself and disappeared. I could work through my situation, rationalizing it in my head, but I couldn't bear to let my heart feel it. I had to desensitize myself from feeling pain from being abandoned, feeling alone, the rape, and where I was going from here, but it was hard to let anyone in.

I told Mom I had to talk to someone, or I would go crazy.

She couldn't have me blabbing to someone, so she found a psychologist named Mrs. Nelson at a private clinic without delay. She was happy to get me off her back, and I was glad to have someone to talk to who would listen for a change.

I saw Mrs. Nelson twice a week until I returned to school in September.

Even though I finally had someone to talk to, I felt more depressed telling her about everything that had transpired. She gave me a prescription for an anti-depressant to make me feel better.

As the weeks passed, she identified many sources of my depression and said it was difficult to pinpoint any one cause.

She told me I had abandonment issues because my birth Mother left me. She also said I had all the typical guilty feelings of a child of alcoholics.

She explained that my guilt about the abortion came from the spiritual bond between the baby and the mother inside the womb. She supposed no one could explain why it happened; it was natural.

She reminded me that there was no going back, only forward. That helped me to let go of an abundance of guilt and shame, but many of my ghosts still haunt me.

"The worst part, Betty, is that you blame yourself for being raped. You have tried for so long to stay out of Bob and Grace's way that you don't think you're worthy of anyone's love. Your nightmares about getting killed show that you feel inadequate, which comes from being abandoned or not being adopted by the Otts. You have little confidence or respect for yourself, which is NOT your fault. My God, It's a good thing you're a survivor. The events of your life have only made you stronger."

Mrs. Nelson gave me a book and some information about children of alcoholics. It is a book called I'm Okay, You're Okay, which is about putting things into perspective and gaining self-esteem. She knew that if I could have some knowledge about what was happening to me, I could learn to overcome it and move on.

Mrs. Nelson had become my solace, and I looked forward to seeing her. I asked her about a recurring nightmare I had for years and wanted to know how to get rid of it.

She asked me if I would consider being hypnotized. Part of me was afraid to find out why I had such bad nightmares, but the other part just wanted them to stop. I was tired of the years of screaming and waking up in a cold sweat, afraid to breathe, so I let her do it. I wasn't prepared for what she uncovered.

"Okay, Betty, close your eyes and concentrate on my voice.

I want you to see yourself as a little girl. You're still in California and very young, playing like little girls do. You're drifting back, going further back and back. Now your arms are getting heavy, very heavy. Your arms feel like bricks, and you can't hold them up."

My arms fall to my sides as I drift away.

"I was four years old and sleeping in the center of a large queen bed in a small dark bedroom. The door leading into my bedroom was an old-fashioned half-light door with a large window in the top half. A small outdoor light shined through the window onto my bed. Three loud knocks on the windowpane awakened me. I sat up, my eyes darting toward the glass."

"I saw the figure of a large, bearded man wearing a black knit fisherman's hat and a plaid shirt. He reminded me of the bully, Brutus from Popeye. Though his face was a silhouette, I could see his rugged, pockmarked face. I was trembling, arms wrapped around my legs, with my knees up to my chest. When he knocked again, I yelled for Mom, but there was no answer. "Mommy, Mommy," I cried as loud as I could. There was no answer, only the sound of music from another room and voices laughing outside. The man wiggled the doorknob, trying to open the door. I stared at the knob crying in fear, terrified that he would get in."

"Suddenly, he opened the door, and the music got louder. I grabbed the cover and brought it over my head, hoping he would only see a crumpled blanket as I laid myself as flat as possible.

In my head, I was praying he would go away. I heard his footsteps approaching me and stopping at the edge of the bed. As he removed my blanket, I saw him towering over me. He smelled like molded food and whiskey. He was filthy: his fingernails and hands were dirty, and his belly hung over his pants. He reached down to me, and all at once, I was floating above my body in the corner of the room, watching the man climb onto me as I disappeared. I gasped for air, screamed, and then I woke up."

"Betty! Are you okay?"

When I nodded, she said, "Where were you in the dream?"

"I was at our old house in San Diego."

"You remember the house in San Diego?"

"Yes, but just bits and pieces. It was a long house with a big tree in the front yard. I had my room."

"You liked it there."

"Yes, I felt unsafe there. My parents would have parties and make me stay in my room. I was scared because I didn't know who everyone was.

"Do you think the dream was just a dream?"

"I used to think it was only a dream, but then as I got older, I realized it may have happened."

"What made you first think that? Was there a specific event?"

"No, I know my parents and how they are. I read a book about floating above your own body. It said the mind protects itself by removing you from trauma."

"You're right; that's probably what happened while you were molested."

"I just don't know how anyone could do that to me. I was so tiny."

She asked if my nightmares were in color. I told her I only had one that I knew was in color.

"In this nightmare, I'm in a different house; it's much nicer, with a stairway inside the front door. I hear loud noises and growls at the front door; as I run down the stairs, I look to my left into the living room, where Mom stands on the other side of the couch. She yells and says, "Don't open that door, don't." "I can see the fear in her eyes, and I smile, then I reach for the door handle and open the door toward the living room. A mean pack of huge dogs runs into the living room, and as they jump over the couch, they attack her. Blood is everywhere as they tear her flesh off her bones. I smile, listening to her screams as I calmly walk back up the stairs."

"Oh my, you must hate your mother. Where do you think that comes from?"

As I summed up my childhood to her, it read like a grocery list of what not to do when you raise a child. I spoke about my need for love and to be hugged, the neglect, the alcohol, the lack of encouragement, the lack of trust, the lack of support, baby bottles, accusations, and my dysfunctional family situation.

"I just wanted to feel loved."

"You think your mom is mostly to blame?"

"I think she has always been jealous of my relationship with Dad."

"What do you mean?"

"She feels he gave me too much. Everything I ever got was shared with the other two families that lived next to us. She treats him like crap."

"How does she do that?"

"She yells at him for every little thing and racks up tabs at grocery stores, bars, and clothing stores so that Dad couldn't retire when he got out of the Navy.

"But your dad drinks as well, doesn't he?"

"Wouldn't you drink if you had to work and listen to my mom all day?"

Mrs. Nelson changed the subject. "Are those the only nightmares you have?"

"No, I have had some that cause me to wake up in pain."

"Really? Where do you feel the pain?"

"I feel it here in my back." I pointed to my kidney area.

"What is it from? Can you describe the dream to me?"

"I was in my nightgown running around my house on Brown Street screaming. I looked behind me, and a man was running after me, trying to stab me with a giant needle. When he stabbed me, I woke up crying and cramping in pain. I couldn't move."

"Why do you suppose you have that dream?"

"I don't know. I don't even know who the man is."

"Have you talked to your parents about any of this?"

"No. They wouldn't believe me anyway."

"You don't think your dad would believe you?"

"I don't know whether he would tell me all this is my fault or all of it is a lie."

"Will you promise me that you will tell them before we talk again? I want to hear their reaction to all this.

You must be strong, Betty. I know you can do it."

"Okay, I'll try."

"You did well today."

I took Mrs. Nelson's advice and sat down with Mom that evening.

"This is bull.

Why are you making all this up? Do you need attention?" snapped Mom.

"I knew this would happen, so I never told you. Whenever I encounter a problem, you say the same thing. I don't know why I even bother." I left the room and didn't bring it up again.

In my next session with Mrs. Nelson, she asked me about their reactions.

I told her, and Mom said I was making it up and blamed it on my needing attention. And I couldn't face Dad after he accused me of getting raped because of my clothing.

During our sessions for the next few weeks, we talked about my friend Joyce and her situation.

"Joyce and I aren't close like before she moved. She can't wait to escape her mother's oppressive, overbearing abuse. May is on welfare and scalps the state money that comes for her children while she gets child support from her absent husband."

"It sounds as if Joyce has serious problems to deal with."

Many times, the kids caught the brunt of her anger in the form of the back of her hand. She relied heavily on her children until they were finally old enough to move out. Once the others escaped to their freedom, Joyce experienced the full effect of her Mother's Huntington's disease and neglect. She cared for her mother during the most intense effects of the disease, even to the extent of writing the checks for the household bills and ensuring they had food. Of course, Joyce always denies that's what happened."

"What about her brother Jimmy?"

"He still lives there, but Joyce says he stays away as much as he can, and May doesn't make him do anything."

"His subtle presence probably shields him to a certain extent, but it sounds as if she's bipolar as well. Her disease and those episodes have a fifty percent chance of being inherited by being transferred to each of her children, and they could already bore the emotional wounds of her sharp tongue."

"I can tell by their actions toward me and each other that May has already stripped them of their self-esteem and worth."

"Why do you say that?"

"Joyce gets overly sensitive if I say something to help her; she says I think I'm better than her. I don't think she loves herself; at the very least, she lacks self-confidence. I spend as much time as I can in the city with Joyce, but she still lives with her mother, so I don't feel like I'm on my own up there except when I'm with my boyfriend, Bobby."

"Are you intimate with him?"

"Of course, I lost my virginity a long time ago. Besides, who's gonna stop me?"

"Aren't you afraid you'll get pregnant?"

"No, we use condoms. Besides, I love him, and that wouldn't be so bad, would it?"

"Yes, it would, Betty. You can't manage your life right now and don't need a baby."

"You don't understand; I need Bobby. He helped me realize I had to let go of Kurt, and even though I think of him often, I knew he was not mature or strong enough to handle where I'd been or needed to go. We drifted farther apart. It couldn't have worked because Kurt was one year younger, so we had to wait three more years before he could leave home. As much as I cared about him, I had to find a guy to help me escape this nowhere town."

"You need to get out before it's too late, but you're too young to fend for yourself. It would be best if you considered foster care. You are strong enough to make it without the Ott's. We wouldn't have any trouble proving they are unfit parents. Please consider it, Betty. You need someone in your life who will help shelter you, protect you, and guide you."

She gave me some phone numbers of agencies that would help me. I was scared to death but had already survived so much at sixteen.

Why did I need a foster parent? Why couldn't I move away from my parents on my own? I could do it. I was used to living on my own anyway. So, I started working on a plan while Mrs. Nelson and I met for sessions twice a week. It turned out that having a "shrink" helped pinpoint some areas of my life hindering me.

I was very blessed to find Mrs. Nelson; she was the only one who didn't try to make me feel worse about my choices. I knew I could depend on her for good advice without judgment. She was able to help me realize the pain I was going through and how to turn my life around. Without her and God, only God knows where I would be.

I started school that fall, but it was short-lived. I chose East Greenwich High, but the kids bullied us, and after what I'd been through, I couldn't handle the petty high school drama. Not feeling safe at school or home, Mrs. Nelson knew it wouldn't be long before I left.

Back then, the law wouldn't allow me to live independently, but I was a determined and *resourceful* sixteen-year-old who would find a way to make it. This proved to be the most challenging and crucial time in my life. After groveling, Joyce's older sister, Susan, finally agreed to let me live with her and Dale, their daughter Sissy, and a malamute Husky in a two-bedroom apartment on Fortner Street. I moved in with my childhood tormentor in December of 1972, but it was better than living with foster parents who would be strangers.

Chapter 15: Consequences of Trust

My most vivid childhood memories of Susan were those huge rollers in her curly brown hair. She was short and had thick, stocky, crusty legs from psoriasis. She looked and acted differently from the rest of the children, and Joyce speculated Susan had another father.

She was always bossy when I was a child, and as the years passed, she'd grown worse.

Susan nagged me daily for no reason that I could tell.

It was apparent she never liked me and probably never would, although I never knew why. So, I did what Susan told me, went to work, and stayed out late often, just at the New York System in Smith Hill.

I have always felt a special bond with Joyce because of how she was treated, and I tried to see her as often as I could, but she also had Mattie.

Joyce introduced me to her shortly after she moved to the city, but there was something about her I didn't like. She thought I was jealous, but mostly, I was just disgusted. The clothes draped from her anorexic frame were wrinkled, dingy, and dirty. Her matted, dull, brown hair looked unkempt.

Her skin tone was uneven, and her teeth were brown. She had lost an eye as a child, so Joyce liked her. Being with someone with a disability helped her feel better about herself and her situation. One of the things I hated most about Mattie was that she gave Joyce pot. She never smoked the stuff until she met Mattie.

On those occasional good days that Mattie was not hanging onto Joyce, we met at the New York System close to the capitol. It was the same conversation almost every day.

We sat at the hot dog place close to the window facing the street, watching people pass by.

"I can't wait to get away from my Motha, she's drivin' me crazy, and I can't take it," Joyce said.

"Why don't you move in with one of your sisters or brothers?"

"Mom won't let me go, and I'm still in school. Besides, they won't let me move in with them because then no one will be theya to take ca of Mom."

"That's bad. Why can't you live with Mattie? Just quit school; that's what I did to escape home."

"I can't, I'm afraid. You know not everyone can do what you do. I thought you were crazy fow just up and leaving like that."

"I had no choice, and it sounds like you have no choice either."

"Wow, look at that guy, over theya in the poc. He's cute and looks like he has a friend."

"Oh yeah, nice."

"Do you wanna go to the poc for a while?"

"No," I said. "I think we should wait for them to come in here. I've seen them in here before, at night."

"That's easy for you to say, you have Bobby, but I have no one."

"I haven't seen Bobby since his ex, Nadine, returned. I was just his rebound, I guess. I'm so sick of guys using me and then throwing me away."

"I'm sorry, I didn't know. Look, theya crossing the street."

"Try to act like you don't see them; you don't want to look desperate, do you?"

"Okay, for right now, we'll stay hea."

"They do look great in their jeans, don't they?"

"Yeah, all that long dark hair and those big dark brown eyes," I said.

"Here they come."

"Okay, play it cool. Let them speak first."

"Hi. Do you girls mind if we sit hea?"

"Who are you?" I asked.

The short one said, "I'm Babe, and this is Frankie." Pointing to his friend.

"What kind of name is Babe?" I asked.

Frankie said, "The girls call him that because he has a baby face, and they love his dimples."

"I get it."

The guys pushed their way onto our seats. Babe sat next to me, and Frankie sat next to Joyce. They were natural charmers, and they knew it.

"So, we play pool at the baa down on the corna once in a while," Babe said.

"Is that an invitation?" Joyce asked.

Frankie said, "Well, I have a girlfriend, but if you wanna come down with her, you can."

"Oh, I see what's happening. You want to talk to Betty." Joyce said.

She didn't realize how embarrassed she made me feel. She never thought about how her actions affected me.

"No, we want to talk to both of you, but Babe doesn't have a girlfriend."

I couldn't help but think, oh wow, could I be his next girlfriend?

He was gorgeous and had double dimples on each cheek when he smiled. His teeth were so beautiful next to his black-as-coal eyes and hair. I could tell he was a smooth talker, so I had to take it slow.

Joyce was very disappointed; I could see it in her eyes, and she couldn't wait to leave.

"Anything you girls need, you just let us know. We can get anything around here, and we have connections." Frankie said.

"What about fake IDs? Can you get me a fake ID so I can work elsewhere other than waitressing?" I asked.

"Why do you need a fake? You must be at least 18, right?" Babe asked.

"No, she isn't," Joyce said sarcastically.

It was an all-too-common look when she wanted to hurt me.

149

"I'm only 16, but I moved away from home. I'm alone and need a better job to get me a place."

"Oh, okay, well, I know someone who can get you what you need," Babe said.

I liked Babe right away and could tell he liked me, too. He, Joyce, and I spent some time getting to know one another at the pool hall. Babe and I even went over to his sister's house for dinner. After about a month, I agreed to go on a date, but I wanted to go slow because I'd already gone through so much with guys.

I floated through the week. I couldn't stop thinking about how genuine Babe seemed. On Saturday, Babe picked me up at Susan's house. He walked me down to his car and opened the door for me. Babe was an absolute gentleman.

"I have to stop at my house to pick up my wallet," he said.

"Would you like to come up and see where I live?"

"No, I'll wait," I said.

"My parents are home; it's okay," he said, leaning over to me.

"Okay, I guess it would be cool to see your house."

He lived on the second floor of a run-down, three-story, New England wood-sided apartment building with one main entrance in the front for all three apartments. The stairwell was dark as we carefully approached the second floor.

Leading me up the stairwell, Babe held my hand so I wouldn't slip. I saw the back of his dad's chair as we entered the living room. It was an old tweed brown rocker recliner. He reclined enough for me to see the bald spot on the top of his head and his faded green t-shirt and work pants. Babe announced me.

"Hey, pops, this is Betty."

His Dad never took his eyes off of the TV. Instead, he grunted in acknowledgment, "Yea, yea," he said, waving his hand.

The room was dark, lit by the light from the TV, and smelled of stale cigarettes. It reminded me of home.

"Ya wanna see my room?" Babe asked.

At first, I hesitated, but then I thought of his dad right outside the door.

Babe closed the door behind me.

"What do you think?" He asked.

"Cozy."

"Cozy enough for a little kiss?" he asked, smiling as he moved closer.

His hand slipped under my hair, and he pulled me closer.

"Babe, we'll miss the movie if we don't hurry."

"The movie can wait. We'll have another chance to see it."

"I think we should go now."

Then he kissed me, running his hands up and down my body.

I pushed him away. "We really should go. I'm hungry, and I want to see the movie." I wasn't starving but felt pressured into doing something I wasn't ready for.

"Just sit down and relax, what's your problem?"

I heard the disappointment in his voice and sat down, but I was nervous now.

I was afraid he would never see me again if I didn't give him what he wanted. What right did I have to say no?

Too insecure after a lifetime of being beaten down, I gave in due to sheer mental weakness. He sat beside me, lowered me onto the bed, and kissed me while unbuttoning my shirt. I protested and pushed him away, saying, "NO!"

"Please, I want to see the movie," I said, pushing his hand away from my breasts. Babe persisted. When I realized what was happening to me, he was pulling off my pants.

"No, please, no." Realizing he wouldn't stop, I said, "Use a condom. Are you going to use something?"

"No, I don't have any. Don't worry; I'll pull out."

He finished quickly, and he didn't pull out in time.

My fear turned into frustration at his and my lack of responsibility. Another man lied to me again. In the end, he got what he wanted. I felt used and embarrassed and asked him to take me home. I was disgusted with myself.

Why didn't I just run? I don't know why I even cared after he treated me like that. I wanted to believe that he liked me after a month together.

As we pulled up in front of Susan's house, I asked, "Will I see you again, Babe?"

"I'll call you." He said, looking at me with a half-smile.

I knew he wouldn't call. For the next two weeks, as my chaotic life advanced ever so slowly, I called his house many times, but he never returned any of my phone calls, so I just accepted that he was done with me and continued with my life.

Joyce met a guy who promised to be her knight in shining armor, Roger Quackenhedge. He was an older man who was tall and skinny with black hair and a face like a zombie: sullen face, high cheekbones, and bulging eyes. I thought he was ugly, but he was fun and genuine.

Roger was friendly enough to find Joyce a studio apartment on the Boulevard. So, at seventeen, she was finally separating from her mother. She found a job across the street at the pizza parlor. It wasn't long before I gladly accepted her offer to move into the tiny studio. We didn't have a bedroom, so we slept on the hide-a-bed couch.

Roger and Joyce argued often, and Joyce nagged me as well, so when Roger and I got an opportunity to teach her a lesson, we grabbed it.

Roger peeked over at me and winked. "It's pretty cold outside with all that snow on the ground. I ought to put your naked ass out on the fire escape.

The second floor has a nice view, Betty.

I made an affirming gesture back at Roger when Joyce wasn't looking. It was a go.

We stripped her down, flung her out on the metal fire escape landing, and locked the window.

Immediately, she started to beg us to let her back in.

"Come on guys, let me in; this isn't funny," she said, shivering with her naked white arms over her freckled body. We stared at her, laughing hysterically through the glass door.

"Well, go downstairs and enter the front door," I said.

"I'm in my underwear! You know I can't do that."

153

We just looked at her, grinning as she shouted her obscenities.

"Do you promise to stop being a bitch?" Roger asked.

"No! I hate you guys! Let me in now!"

"Then you're not coming in yet. You gotta promise not to be an annoying nag anymore!" I said.

"Please let me in! It's cold out here. I'm gonna freeze to death. Please."

"Promise you won't gripe at us anymore about the little stuff, and we will let you in.".," said Roger.

"Okay, okay. I promise.

Please let me in. I am freezing my ass off out here."

"Too late, it's already gone!" I said, laughing.

We let her back in, but she didn't want to talk to us afterward. She sent Roger home and ignored me for the rest of the evening, which wasn't an entirely bad thing. Another time, I closed her up on the hide-in-bed couch after she got onto me for not making the bed. I was running late, and she had nagged me until I couldn't take it anymore. After she said she was sorry, I let her out, but you would think she would learn to be more content after that fiasco. She was a glutton for punishment. Joyce often took pleasure in seeing how far she could antagonize a situation. And it gave her a unique sense of control when she could say, "I told you so."

I had been working odd jobs until now, everything from housekeeping to waitress work at the local restaurant. It had been months since I heard from Bob or Grace. Now that I had a new home and license, I needed a better job, but it would have to be within walking distance since I didn't have a car.

I found work at the Armbrust Chain Factory six blocks away. It was piecework, but when I went over quota, I made $6.00 an hour, which was good money back then. Linking jewelry chains under a magnifying glass is tedious, but it was a job, and they had benefits. After all, I didn't even have a high school education.

I was stressed and didn't think much of it when I missed a period. I wasn't used to working these many hours. I tried to dismiss my fears but had never been three weeks late. I told Joyce.

She said, "Well, wait anotha two weeks, and then we'll see a docta. I can show you whea the free clinic is."

A few days later, I started getting sick.

A couple more weeks passed, and Joyce told me, "You should go to the clinic; you could be pregnant. I don't know why you weren't more caful. You wouldn't have to deal with this now if you didn't get out of the car in the first place."

I could hear a familiar "I told you so" in her voice.

She always got such power from pointing out my mistakes.

What in the world was I going to do if I was pregnant? I had nothing going for me and no support system in place.

"Joyce, can you please come with me to the clinic? I'm not sure how to get there on the bus."

"Betty, I have to go to work this aftanoon, and I need some sleep."

"I don't feel good, and I'm nervous. Please come with me; we'll be back in plenty of time."

"I can't; I have to work. Don't be such a baby, Betty."

"I'm not being a baby; Joyce, I could be pregnant. Don't you get it? The notion of having another life depending on me when I can hardly make ends meet scares the shit out of me. I would go with you if you needed me to. I can wait until you have some time off with me."

Joyce said, "When I have time off, I want to spend time with Roga, not the entire day at the clinic."

 It was a dreary day in April of 1973 when I stepped off the bus in front of the free clinic. The well-known Women and Infants Free Clinic was a tall, plain, square brick building, nothing unusual. It was notorious for being one of the largest abortion clinics in the state. Ironically, the same place that helped care for babies also helped eradicate them discreetly. I walked through the glass doors to what could have been an ordinary clinic waiting area, except for the despair that loomed above each girl. The stone-faced receptionist only added to the dismal clinic ambiance. They had seen so many young girls come in; they became desensitized that I was lost and desperately needed to speak to someone who could tell me what to do.

At sixteen, I expected to be the youngest girl there, but some looked barely fourteen. Young girls in dirty jeans with tear-stained faces avoided eye contact with anyone. I longed to reach out to them and help, but I knew I couldn't. I just looked down at the well-worn tiled floor, away from all that sadness, and waited for them to call me. The air stunk; a dead, musty scent mixed with antiseptic. I ran to the bathroom and threw up my crackers.

I had a lump in my throat, desperate to keep the tears at bay.

It's me; I'm here; this is not a nightmare. For 4 hours, I waited in disbelief before someone called me back to one of the rooms.

I gave them a pee sample, and 30 minutes later, a doctor came in to deliver my nightmare.

"You're pregnant, about two months, as far as I can tell."

I was in shock only briefly before I could no longer contain myself. I started to sob. The doctor was unfazed as he began his examination.

"So, you want an abortion then?"

I opened my mouth to speak but couldn't utter a word. Instead, I hesitated.

"I need to think about this for a few minutes."

"Take your time but get dressed because we'll need this room." He said as he shut the door behind him.

I put my head into my hands and cried. I needed more time to think about this. How could I make such a decision in just a couple of minutes?

But then again, I needed to find out where I would get my next meal. How could I even think of bringing another person into this world? I was confused and felt so alone because I didn't have anyone to turn to for advice that had gone through this. I wondered if this is what my birth mother went through with me. Was it this hard for her, too? Did she sit in a clinic and feel the same desperation? I wanted to call her for help. But I knew she didn't want me or my problems.

A nurse came in and suggested I see the hospital social worker.

She gave me her room number and said her name was Mrs. Antonio.

"She can help you make a decision. Even if you don't want an abortion, you can still put the child up for adoption."

"I don't know if I could do that. I couldn't handle my child being out there looking for me and not knowing where or who I was. I went through that and couldn't put my child through the same thing."

"Alright, just keep the door open when you leave." She nodded and closed the door behind her.

I left the clinic, not knowing where to go; I wandered around the city until it was almost dark. People rushed around me to get home and out of the humid spring air, but I was so numb I couldn't feel anything. Hours later, I was still confused about what to do. I should've gone to see Mrs. Antonio, but I didn't think she could help me.

I was on my own now. I called Babe's house again, but his father said he wasn't home. So many things flashed in my head all at once. I didn't even know how I got to the other side of the city or how many buses I had to catch to get back to the apartment; it was all a blur. My bloodshot eyes burned from crying so much.

When I finally arrived, Joyce was in the kitchen making tea.

"What happened? What did the clinic say? Are you pregnant?"

I looked up at her, trying to be strong, but I could only get one word in before I lost it again.

"Yes." Sobbing uncontrollably.

"Oh my God, Betty, what aa ya gonna do?"

"I don't know yet. This is like my worst nightmare is coming true."

"What aa yowa mom and dad gonna say?"

"That's not the worst of it. I don't even know if I will keep the baby yet. They don't have to find out if I don't keep the baby."

"Aa, you thinkin' about anotha abortion?"

"Joyce, the first abortion wasn't my fault."

"Yeah, but you still had one."

"I know, I hated it; it was horrible."

"What about finding a better job and finishing school? How ya gonna go back to school with a kid?"

"How am I gonna support a child without a father?"

Over the next two hours, Joyce and I discussed my possibilities over tea. I knew it would be better to abort the baby because I wouldn't have any future if I kept it. We decided that Susan might be able to help since she had her daughter out of wedlock.

We took a bus to Susan's house the following weekend to see what advice she could give me.

When I told her what happened, she said, "I'm not surprised this happened.

What's wrong with you? Didn't you take birth control?"

"Didn't you hear anything I said? He took what he wanted no matter what I said."

Joyce looked at Susan with that "Yeah, right" look.

"Mom never mentioned anything about that. Sex was never mentioned in our house. Besides, I had no choice."

"You had a choice? Betty, from how you've described it, you could have left. He pressured you, and you fell for it. Now your motha is gonna blame me for this."

"What? Why would Mom blame—"

"—Well, think about it, you were living with me. What aa you gonna do about it? When aa you going to tell Grace?"

"I don't know if I'm gonna tell her."

"You'll have to if yuaa gonna keep this baby."

I broke down again, not knowing what I should do. Susan hadn't been much help, but I knew she was right. I had to take responsibility for what had happened. I needed some more time to think it through. Could I put myself and another baby through another abortion? On the other hand, did I have any right to bring a child into my life when I could hardly feed myself? No one had ever loved me unconditionally; would I be capable of love?

Chapter 16: Alone, I Turn to My Heart

I was amidst a cultural movement supporting bold ideas and women's equality. Our country was beginning to implement these new ideas, while the older generation desperately clung to the old ways and needed to be more supportive.

Every door was closed to me except one, the despairing door back to my broken childhood.

I embarked on the journey to search for my apartment. Joyce and Roger always talked about moving out independently, and I always felt like I was in the way. I called Mom in Narragansett and asked if I could come for the weekend. I had no idea how I would tell her, but I knew I had to, no matter how it turned out. She agreed to pick me up the following Saturday morning. As I waited for her, I could barely contain my nervousness. I was glad I was only two months pregnant and not yet showing.

She pulled up in the Nova, and I got in. I could feel her watching me as I fumbled with my bag. I stared out the window as she pulled away, hoping to avoid her eyes. I kept our conversation generic. We talked about jobs and friends and how I was doing. I told Mom about Joyce's plans and that I would need to get my bedroom furniture as soon as I found an apartment. She reminded me I was not eighteen yet and couldn't do anything. Without going into detail, I said,

"Well, I'm seventeen now and have my apartment and a job."

I didn't mention the ID and was afraid to say anything about the pregnancy because, although Susan was against an abortion, she was not quite in favor of *me* keeping the baby. I needed someone in my corner. I knew my life would never be the same, but maybe that's what I needed.

God knew my life up to this point had been lousy. Maybe this baby would be my blessing, not the curse that others told me it would be.

Perhaps, for once, I would know the kind of love I never had from people who should've been there for me.

When we arrived at the house, I walked to Roxanne's, thinking I could get a fresh look at my problem, being careful not to mention anything about abortion. She was a year younger than I and even though she was wise beyond her years, she was still  naive about worldly problems. She was in school and went to church all the time. I didn't want her to think I was the person her mother said I was. Although she never knew about the abortion I already had, I thought she might have some advice I hadn't thought of. As we walked along the seawall, Roxanne seemed genuinely concerned.

"Roxanne, what am I gonna do about this mess?"

"Have you told Grace yet?"

"No, I'm afraid she won't understand."

"Understand that you felt pressured into having sex? It happens all the time. It happened to me with Phillip."

"Oh, my God. Did you?"

"No, he's a pig. I just got out of the car as soon as I could."

"I was so afraid that I couldn't run. I wanted to, but I didn't and said no."

"They don't care what you say. You can say no all day, but if you run, they'll get the message."

"Why didn't you tell me about this before?"

"It never came up."

"What do I do, Roxanne? I feel so alone, and I know Grace will blame me."

"Yeah, but Betty, it is your fault because you didn't run."

"Should I keep the baby or give it up?"

"I suggest you move back home from the city and finish school.

How will you support this baby?"

"I'll work."

"With no education? Are you crazy?"

It was easy for her to think like a girl who spends time with church friends and can make it in school. Small towns have no mercy. A pregnant teen was a good target, running my name into the dirt every day, and she wasn't pregnant. It became apparent to me that she wouldn't be able to understand my situation.

Cold sea spray gusted over the sea wall, so we couldn't stay long.

On the way back to her mom's apartment, things were almost silent. We were both mulling over the details of the conversation, waiting for a revelation.

I would be in limbo if I kept the baby and damned if I didn't. Terminating the pregnancy *would* allow me to finish my education, get a good job, and maybe one day have a child after I settle down.

163

*Terminating the pregnancy...*Those words sent a tremble through my body.

Roxanne and I hugged goodbye and promised to keep in touch. We caught up with each other later that year. I left Roxanne's house and walked back toward the beach. I felt no relief. The more people I spoke to, the more confused I was. Most wanted me to get rid of the baby, but how many of these people had babies? Grace never *was* the motherly type; Roxanne focused on her academics and church matters and didn't have a child, nor did Joyce. Susan was the only one who thought I shouldn't get an abortion.

On Sunday morning, I awoke to rays of sunshine radiating through my window. I got up, made breakfast, and waited for Susan to arrive on the porch. She arrived just before noon, and we sat on the porch, discussing how I would break the news. Grace finally ventured out with her coffee and morning cigarette.

Susan nudged me and said, "Grace, Betty has something to tell you."

I stared sternly at Susan and then looked away as if to say *we don't have to approach it like that!*

"Why are you two acting so strange? What's going on?" Mom said.

Okay... here goes. "Mom, I'm pregnant, and before you start yelling, we should talk first."

She was surprised but not stunned. "I had a feeling something like this would happen in the city. Okay, we'll have to take care of it."

"What do you mean? Are you talking about abortion? What if I want to keep this baby?"

"Betty, you can't keep that child; you are too young! What about school? Do you even know who the father is?"

"Of course I do; what's that supposed to mean?" I said.

Susan said, "You know Grace, and she can get help to raise this baby- she doesn't have to do it alone."

"You mean welfare?" Looking at me, she said, "Your father is going to hit the roof."

"It's not your decision; it's mine," I said.

"You're not old enough to make your own decisions. Don't expect us to help you raise that baby."

"I never did. Don't you think it's too late to be upset about my decisions? They have always been *my* decisions because God knows you never made any good decisions *for* me."

Susan got up and went into the house. Grace sat beside me and said, "Get the abortion and go back to school, make something of yourself. Ginny was right when she said you would never amount to anything."

She looked at me to see my reaction.

"You are so stupid and make such dumb mistakes, Betty."

I looked at her with angry tears, "Why are you being so horrible to me? Why can't you understand and accept me for who I am?"

"It wasn't my fault you went off and got pregnant again," Grace said smugly.

I said, "Wait a minute, the first time I was raped, and you still blame me for that, right? If you weren't drunk that night, I wouldn't have been raped and wouldn't have had to move out into the city." I got up and brushed the dirt off my pants. "OOOOH…Why do I even bother? You never loved me anyway."

Grace said, "How can you say that? We took you when your *mother* gave you up. We fed, clothed, and provided you with a home."

"You fed me hotdogs, cheeseburgers, and maybe a meal occasionally, but I had to cook it myself most of the time. And you call this apartment a home?" I continued, my voice getting louder. "I went to work at the stables when I was twelve to buy things for myself. I didn't get my bed until I was nine, and you say you loved me?

You've always envied me and were jealous of my relationship with Dad!"

"What are you talking about? I was *never* jealous, and you're imagining things." I took a deep breath, and as I walked away, I said, "That's okay. I'll figure this out myself just like I have everything else."

She asked again, "Would you at least consider an abortion? Think about this child; it won't have anything. You're broke, and where's the father? You don't have a way to raise this baby."

I said, "I already feel love for this baby, which is more than I ever got from you, so yes, this baby will be loved, and I will provide everything I can to support it."

I was startled to hear myself. I was unsure what to do, but faced with Mom's reality and her belief that I was doomed to fail, I became determined to prove them all wrong.

Mom continued, "What kind of job could you possibly get without finishing school?"

"I'll go back to school; I can make this work. I know I can."

Dad would be home from the bar soon; he usually came in around 2 p.m. to get some sleep. I was exhausted and not feeling well after arguing with Mom, so I went back in the house and lay on my old bed to prepare for round two and the war about to ensue. I knew she would try to fill his ear full of propaganda before I could even get in a word.

I heard Dad come in around 2:30, and right away, Mom followed him in and got the first jab. I wanted to explain what I was feeling and going through myself, but Mom made it sound so bad that I ran out of the house quietly with Susan without telling him anything. I could feel his disappointment pouring out over me as she continued. I didn't want to rub salt on old wounds.

Susan and I left the pier that afternoon. I'd outgrown my childhood and was no longer welcome there. Was I ever their daughter? No adoption, no court proceedings. I never was their daughter. Are parents supposed to be fair-weather parents? Is love always conditional? I was never going to belong.

Chapter 17: Emancipated Dependent

Joyce and Roger moved out together, so I found a place to live on the other side of Narragansett Boulevard. My new apartment was on a little side street called Sassafras, eight blocks from the factory.

It was an old, majestic, three-story New England house with living room bay windows. Directly through the front door was an enormous room, and on the other side was a formal dining area. It was a partially furnished place with a couch, table, chairs, and a twin bed in each room, but there was still a lot of gaping space. The ceilings were twelve feet high, and the kitchen cabinets were too tall to reach without a stool. But the original wood floors were beautiful. The dining room led to two bedrooms. It was in a bad neighborhood but a steal at a few hundred a month.

Considering my fresh start, I did a little housecleaning in other areas. I just turned seventeen in April and was already two months pregnant, and this was my fourth address in a year. It was time to get some things established.

Living alone was more challenging than I imagined, plus I was sick every day, but there was no way I was going back. The crackers I ate in the morning were all I could afford to buy, and they didn't stop the nauseous feeling. At least I had eight blocks to get it all out while I walked to work every morning. My boss was getting upset that I was sick all day long and had to move my worktable closer to the bathroom so I could make it to the toilet. He said I should consider quitting if I couldn't do the job. He threatened to take my job away a few times.

I had not made any friends at work, and Joyce lived too far away from me to visit. I was alone, scared, and struggling to make ends meet with the utilities, but I knew I would die if I stood still. I fought to maintain my sanity during the day and cried every night for my baby and myself.

I kept all my appointments at the free clinic, which was hard because I always left there feeling like a piece of meat. The doctors used me as a guinea pig to teach their interns. I would watch them through splayed legs as they crowded around the examining table.

Once they left, I would roll over, grasp the sheet to my chest, and weep.

The only good thing about the clinic was Mrs. Antonio; she and I became good friends, which made visits a little easier. She always made time for me, and often, she would buy me lunch. I confided in her, telling her intimate details about my life. I don't know what I would've done without meeting her.

Pete and Sara, two people living downstairs from me, asked if they could move in and away from all the drama. It was a great way to have money to eat, so I said yes. By my fourth month, I felt confident that I was starting to get things under control. Then the pain started. Sara found me in bed after what seemed like hours and called the ambulance. When they finally arrived, the paramedics started me on an IV drip, put me on a gurney, brought me down the stairs, and drove to St Joseph's Hospital. By the time we arrived, I could talk, and when the doctor came in, he had somehow found out my age and refused to treat me.

"I can't do anything to help you because you are a minor. I need your parents' permission to do a physical and some tests to ensure you're not losing the baby."

I started sobbing. "You have to help me. I can't lose this baby, please! I'm an orphan anyway; my parents want nothing to do with me."

I explained that I had my apartment and job and was living independently. The Dr. insisted I call one of my parents or I would have to leave the hospital. As soon as he left, one of the nurses came in and said,

"Would you like me to help you call anyone? You shouldn't take a chance with these pains?" I gave her Grace's phone number.

A few minutes later, the doctor said, "Your mother called and gave her permission over the phone and said she would be here shortly to sign the papers."

I sobbed, "No, I don't want to see her. Do I have to see her?"

"No, you don't have to see her, but she does have to give her permission because you're a minor. You're suffering from malnutrition and severe dehydration, and your electrolytes are severely unbalanced. You're lucky to be alive, young lady. Are you trying to kill yourself?" asked the doctor in disbelief.

"No sir, I go to the Free Clinic for my pregnancy checkups. I've been getting sick and can't keep anything down."

"Listen, if you don't get extra help with your pregnancy, you will certainly lose this baby."

"But I don't have any money to do that. I barely have enough money to eat!"

"If you don't start eating better and stop working so many hours on your feet, you will have a miscarriage."

After he walked out, I had time to think. I knew I didn't want to lose the baby, but how could I quit my job? I certainly wouldn't eat better if I did that. That doctor didn't live in the real world if he would give me that kind of advice. He probably couldn't live a day in my shoes if his life depended on it.

It's not that I didn't want to get help for my baby's well-being, but everywhere I turned left more indecision in my head. The church sent unwed mothers to group homes where they stayed until giving birth. The babies went into foster care or were adopted.

I was barely seventeen and not married. What chance would I have of keeping it if I went to them?

Then there was the Salvation Army, but they were not readily available and had few homeless shelters. Teaching facilities and programs to help pregnant teens weren't developed because society had not come to terms with the rising population of unwed pregnancies. The numbers were tripling yearly, and according to the government, unwed pregnancy was an issue between the pregnant girl and her parents.

The doctor had taken Mom aside and explained the severity of the situation to her. For the first time in my life, I felt as if she was genuinely concerned for me. She didn't want me to lose the baby. *Maybe a part of her regretted never being able to have a baby herself. Or perhaps she was secretly resentful of me for having a baby; after all, she was worried about how people looked at her. She couldn't have my baby's death on her hands,* I thought to myself. She hesitantly stepped into my room and asked me how I was doing.

"I'm better now," I said, avoiding eye contact.

"Listen, Betty, the doctor told me that if you don't start eating right and get some rest, you'll lose the baby."

171

"Yeah, I know," I mumbled.

"Why don't we return to your apartment and get some things so you can return to the house for a while?"

I started to cry. "Mom, I don't want to go back there. I don't feel welcome there."

"Betty, do you want to lose the baby?"

"Of course not."

"You don't have a choice because you're not eighteen. Besides, what do you think will happen if you stay where you are now?"

I knew she was making sense. Part of me was thinking, *there is no way in hell I'm moving back in with those people*, but the other part of me was struggling to do the right thing for my baby.

I was determined to put my feelings aside for the sake of my child.

The more I thought about my bleak circumstances, the more I knew it was the only option. I hesitantly agreed, but Bob and Grace had already proven their inability to be responsible and loving parents, and I would not let them influence my child to feel the way I did growing up. My baby would not have feelings of inadequacy and rejection from a lack of praise. I would be gone if I could afford to leave that house!

The drive home was deafeningly silent. Neither mom nor I spoke a single word, and strangely, I could not even hear the sound of the car's engine or the traffic around us. As the outside world silently flooded past, all I could hear was my heart pounding in my chest, each beat ticking off the seconds until I faced the inevitable confrontation with my father. The silence would soon be over.

I tried formulating a rational and sympathetic cover story explaining this mess to my father's satisfaction. Maybe if I could spin the facts the right way, my dad would take pity upon me, slump his shoulders, bow his head, and open his arms to embrace me in an all-forgiving hug. He could also go out and buy me a house. Neither event was likely to happen. When I became pregnant, I transcended the minor problems that little girls face with their parents and entered the real world of adult dilemmas.

I got out of the car and reluctantly walked towards the front door.

It was reminiscent of one of those old prison movies where the death row inmate takes his final steps down the long hallway toward his death. As he passes each cell, the other convicts whisper, "Dead man walking." I tried to steal myself for the execution of my sentence. As soon as I walked inside the front door, I saw my father, arms folded, filling the entrance to the kitchen. He looked straight at my belly and then up at my face before turning to Mom in a rage.

"What in the hell is she doing here? I thought I told you she was not welcome here anymore and not to bring her home," he yelled, ignoring my presence in the same room.

Mom tried to calm him, "Bob, the doctor said she might die, and her baby would certainly not live if I left her in the city. He said she was our responsibility during her pregnancy because she is a minor."

Dad interrupted, his voice getting louder, "She made her bed! She left here to make her own decisions, and she can face the consequences. She doesn't need us anymore, remember?"

Provoked, I tried to defend myself, "I don't want to be here anymore than you want me here!" I said calmly to him.

173

Mom held up her hand to me as if to say shut up for a second and then started in on Dad again. "I can't just leave her there to die! Look, it's our responsibility to care for her because if she dies under eighteen, people will blame us."

Mom knew Dad well and knew what cards to play in an argument. She knew how much sway his friends' opinions would carry. He jealously guarded his reputation within his tight circle of friends. He didn't mind being the head of an alcoholic, dysfunctional family just so long as no one knew about it.

Dad hesitated, his eyes squinting, and fell silent. He was evaluating the more significant consequences of his actions and how they would affect them as if he were playing out several chess moves in his head, moving pieces many steps ahead to foresee the likely outcomes of various strategies. He looked back at me, pointed his finger, and said in a measured tone, as if each word were a complete sentence, "Don't think you're gonna stay here. You'll have to move out as soon as you have this baby." He stormed into his room and slammed the door behind him.

That went well, I thought to myself sarcastically. At least Mom seemed to come to my defense and take my side. Yet, as surprising as her actions had been, I knew I would not receive anything but the barest of assistance from my parents; they would provide me with a roof over my head but offer no guidance or emotional support. Although only seventeen years old, I was an adult now and, as such, would have to establish my true path alone.

Chapter 18: Big Disappointments and Small Changes

Living back in their apartment made me sick to my stomach. It wasn't just morning sickness. I had a lot of time to think about getting out of there. I decided to find my old boyfriend, Bobby Calgaricci. I found out he was in prison for four months in Dewitt, Va. I had to find a way out of Narragansett; he could be a good father, marry me, and be a family together. We wrote for a couple of weeks, after which he invited me to stay at his brother's house until he got out. I took a train to  Virginia to see him, hoping he would help me. I believed he still loved me and would offer to marry me even though the baby wasn't his.

Bobby's sister-in-law took less than 5 minutes to lay down the law. When we first met, she was nice; even their seven children were kind to me, maybe because they thought I wasn't staying. I was grateful to finally be in a place where I could get along with ordinary people.

Bobby's older brother and his wife were unhappy that Bobby's pregnant girlfriend would live in their house. I did laundry and dishes and helped to clean the whole house. The teenage children that lived there never lifted a finger to help me. It was remarkable that, physically, I survived.

Emotionally, however, I was a wreck.

175

Within a month of my arrival, I found some letters from Bobby to Nadean that said he would take care of things so they could be together. He was stringing me along by telling me one thing and her another. I was through here and stayed as long as I did because I didn't want to run home with my tail between my legs. There comes a time in everyone's life when Crow is the soup of the day.

Mom,

I'm writing because things here in Virginia are not going well. I know you and Dad helped pay for me to come here, but right after I arrived, Mrs. Calgaricci made it clear I was to cook, clean, and watch her kids. She always goes out with men while her husband drives over the road.

I'm so depressed, and I'm always sick. I don't know what to do. Can you please send me some money to get home? Please! Bobby no longer wants me around, and I think they will kick me out.

They all hate me here. I don't have any money saved because I can't work.

I've been their slave, doing everything for all of them, and they mistreat me. We played a baseball game today, and I stood at one of the bases. One of the big kids slid into my base and stepped on my ankle on purpose, and they all laughed while I cried.

I can't stay here anymore, Mom, please come and get me or send me some money for the train. I Love You, Betty

She told me she didn't understand why I couldn't get my life together. She said, "Not everything is about you. Your father and I have been getting along great, and our lives are much better without you."

I couldn't believe what I was reading. I felt like the other woman in their lives.

Did she hate me that much?

She continued, "Betty Lee, you can't just expect me to drop everything and cater to your every whim? I have a life, too. You have to be responsible and stand on your own now. We are not responsible for you anymore; you made your choice."

As I finished reading, I slowly put the letter beside me and started to weep; I journeyed back to the letter I got from my natural mother. It was sticky hot in Dewitt, and I was miserable, depressed, and crying all the time. It was now that I felt utterly unloved. Everyone around me believed I was worthless. My situation was hopeless, and I felt alone and lost.

Walking into the bathroom, I stared at myself in the mirror. My eyes were swollen and red from crying. How could I continue living on this earth knowing I was unloved and not welcome anywhere, including my home? I opened the cabinet and took inventory of all the pills. I wasn't sure they would do the job. I had made one wrong decision after another, and I couldn't bear it to worsen.

I saw some razors and thought, *I can do that. I'll leave them with a mess I don't have to clean up. I took a straight razor blade from the container and put it on my wrist. The battle in my mind was raging. One side was telling me I should've never been born; I had no right to live and make everyone's life so difficult. The other side was telling me I couldn't do it because if I failed, I would look even more pathetic in everyone's eyes.*

"Oh, come on. One swift cut, and it's all over. No more pain or rejection. Just do it."

"You don't want to do this, Betty. Think about your baby."

"Yea, right. You can't support this child. The baby's gonna starve, and even if it doesn't starve to death, it will still live around the same people you grew up with. The child doesn't have a chance."

Betty, it will hurt a lot if you do it.

You're going to feel pain, and you're destroying another life along with your own. It's not just you anymore. This child can have a chance if you continue to be strong. You can do it; don't give up.

I would fall asleep into nothingness and never wake up. I wouldn't have to endure any more pain anymore. I was mad and disgusted with myself. Why couldn't I die? Do it, Betty, do it!

Blood was everywhere, and just then, I panicked. I held my wrist and grabbed a towel to stop it.

"I'm so weak that I don't have enough strength to kill myself. I cried violently for hours, but my unrelenting cries landed on deaf ears."

I heard the kids returning from the softball game and arguing outside the bedroom door. I didn't want anyone to find me and take me to the hospital. It would be one more failure for them to flaunt.

Exhausted, I rolled myself off the bed and went to the phone. I had to get out of here if I couldn't kill myself. My indecision was like being in a maze. If I take a right, I might end up down a long, winding dead-end, but if I take a left, I may find my way out. If I stayed in Dewitt, I could end up dead. Taking my own life would be equivalent to jumping out of a high-rise window to keep from being burned. If I did survive the fall, I would be broken and emotionally disfigured. I was standing amid two evils and still had no idea which way to go to gain control over my own life.

I had to try again to get my mother to pick me up. I had to admit she was my only option. Grace's pending decision to come for me was the only miracle I could hope for now. That miracle would have to contradict everything in her character and all she had written in her letter to me.

I had no pride left, so I wasn't worried about what Grace would say to me when I called her. I knew what she would say when I put my feelings on the table for her to cut up. I begged her with everything in me for her to let me come back home.

"Why do you always return when you have nowhere else to go? How many times do we have to take you in? What is wrong with you?"

"Mom, I have to come home, or I will end up on the street."

"Once again, she said, "Your Dad and I have been getting along great since you left.

Things are much better here without you."

"These people are heartless, and my baby might die here!" I begged her.

"You have to help me, PLEASE!"

Mom finally gave in, saying, "This is it! You have to grow up. You come home and find a place to go with that child because we can't keep saving you every time you fail. You have to stand up on your own feet."

The following Saturday morning, she picked me up.

Surprisingly, we didn't have a fight or an argument. We said very little to each other. I knew in my heart how Grace felt…I wasn't good for anything except for causing them heartache.

I was dreading seeing Dad. When we arrived home, I braced myself for a fight, but he didn't yell; instead, he handed me a wedding ring.

"You *will* wear this. And you'll get your ass in secretarial school. It's time you made something of yourself, if not for us or yourself, for that baby."

A few weeks later, I did just that. I enrolled in a secretarial school sponsored by a state organization called CEDA. October brought calmer to the house, and I made amends with Dad. I started to see Dr. O'Neil for my prenatal care, which was covered under my dad's medical insurance since I was still a minor. I was getting good care and was starting to feel healthy again.

By Halloween, I was four days past my due date. Mom was more nervous about the labor than I was, so she called Susan to visit for a few days to monitor my progress. She arrived a couple of days before I had my baby and watched over me closely to make sure I was not doing anything to hurt myself or show any signs of labor problems. On November 6th, I awoke to sharp pain in my back and upper abdomen. When I stood up, I felt a warm, wet trickle. I woke Susan, and she confirmed that I was beginning to break my water.

She yelled for Grace, and a few minutes later, we were on our way to the hospital.

Twelve hours later, I watched as my seven lb., 1/4oz baby girl was born. She was crying before she was entirely out.

When the doctor placed my beautiful daughter on my stomach, I fell in love for the first time. How could I have ever considered not having her? I experienced every happiness, sadness, fear, and delight I've ever had. The nurse took her out of delivery, where Mom and Dad awaited the news. Dad looked at her huge, round brown eyes and fell to pieces. "She is so beautiful. Oh, look at those big brown eyes, isn't she beautiful!" he said.

I named my daughter Tracy Marie after a popular song playing over the airwaves back then. For the next three days, I was in the hospital; the nurses made it clear that my single status bothered them. They were rude and rough when they handled me. It wasn't five hours after my delivery that one nurse made me get out of bed after having a saddle block. She told me to get up and stop being lazy.

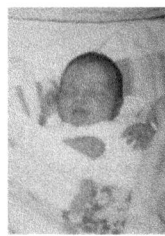

"It's time to walk. You have to get up," she said harshly.

I pulled myself out of bed and stood for 3 minutes before collapsing back into my bed. I had a migraine headache for two weeks.

I couldn't breastfeed because they gave me a Rhogam shot after I gave birth. The doctor told me it went directly into my bloodstream, so they started me on pills that would dry up my milk. I was poison to my new daughter. I didn't have any guidance about how to care for Tracy, and no one ever taught me how to use cocoa butter for stretch marks. Wrapping Tracy in a blanket was second nature, but there were many things I learned as we grew together.

The hospital stay's highlight was when Kurt visited Tracy and me.

He stood at the bottom of my bed, astonished and curious. Curious about what had become of me.

We had little to say; neither wanted to go down a dead-end path by regurgitating old feelings.

He asked, "How do you feel? Are you okay?"

"Sure, I'm fine now, except I can't get up because I have a bad headache."

"Is there anything I can get for you?"

This small talk went on for about 10 minutes, and then he left, wishing me good luck.

I still think of him today and wonder what would've come from staying with him. I had to snap out of it and bring myself back to reality. I have a baby now and had to accept responsibility for her. Guys were no longer at the top of the list for me.

Living with my parents with a new baby was stressful, with their unsolicited advice on how to raise my child as if they knew. Dad worked at night; they wanted the baby to sleep all day so she wouldn't make any noise. I encouraged her to stay awake at night. I had to keep her from crying to avoid disturbing them.

They were forcing me to spoil her, and I was so exhausted from not sleeping. I forged on, day after day, knowing that something had to break for me to make it. I had to get the hell out of there so Tracy could be on my schedule, or I would scream.

Chapter 19: Into the Unknown

I found a neat little apartment on Caswell Street in January of 1974. It was a one-bedroom studio apartment. It had a small bathroom, a kitchenette, and a modest bedroom. Although it was small, it was perfect for Tracy and me. The owners renovated the old house into four apartments with a common area at the entrance on the main floor. The winding staircase led to another landing, like a long hall in a house that joined all the rooms.

It wasn't long before I met the neighbors. Two bikers lived on the main floor, a married couple lived across the hall from them, and another single woman with a son lived across from me on the second floor.

Every weekend was a party, and after being so quiet all the time, it was nice not to have to worry about my music. Tracy's crib was on the opposite side of the wall from the stereo, and she quickly acclimated to the vibrations coming through the wall.

That kid could sleep through anything.

I must admit that the bikers were initially intimidating, especially Harry, with his large, burly frame, wiry beard, and bald head.

He was the ultimate vision of what a biker or a Viking would look like. The same guy that had bitten the heads off the fish would hold Tracy, two months old at this time, like a delicate vase. He was a gentle giant, a great friend, and a protector.

Every so often, he'd suddenly get serious and offer to make an honest woman out of me. He worried about me but never interfered or made me feel like I wasn't doing a good job with my daughter. Harry knew I didn't have those feelings for him and that he would never be more than a good friend.

Harry had a twenty-year-old friend named Daniel who would come down occasionally. He was a biker as well, but not as fierce. He was more of a weekend enthusiast than a true biker. Of course, you can't be too stern in the investment banker field.

Daniel had some money and a condominium in Braintree, Massachusetts. He took up with me right away, and we spent some time together in my apartment one weekend during one of his visits. He invited me to see his place and meet his mom, and I agreed.

That weekend was terrific. We rode the trains and shopped at some of the best stores in Boston.

He bought me a few trinkets, and Tracy got some new outfits. I could see in his eyes how much he cared for her and me. By Sunday afternoon, I knew our time together was ending, and I had to return home to my life. He took me into his parents' living room, where all the fancy chandeliers and curtains were hanging perfectly. We sat on the couch in front of a beautiful tea set on a glass tabletop.

He surprised me, taking my hand and looking into my eyes.

"Marry me, Betty."

I caught my breath. Letting it out slowly, I said, "What did you say?"

"We should get married. I can take care of you and Tracy."

"Wow. Daniel. I mean, this is unexpected. Oh my God, are you serious?"

"Come on, you know I'm crazy about you and Tracy. You could have a great life here with me. You won't have to worry about money, and you'll have a stable place to live."

184

"I don't know you well enough to marry you, Daniel. I'm sorry-- I don't--love you."

"You'll learn to love me. Think about Tracy. We have so much fun together. Can't you think it over?"

His offer was tempting. I could escape from my parents and be with a man who cared for us. But I didn't love him. Ultimately, Tracy and I were on an all-expenses paid trip back home. It was a solemn trip as I questioned myself about my choices.

I could hardly enjoy the freedom living in my apartment should have brought me. Instead, my parents were always at the door. Suddenly, they were concerned parents. I needed to learn how to handle this new attention from them.

I was starting to get cabin fever once again…I felt a change in the wind and had to find a place to escape. We left our studio apartment when Tracy was only four months old.

Mom was still in touch with Dave and Judy, who used to live upstairs from us on Brown Street. They live in Lake Milton, Ohio, now. I called, and they accepted. I bought a bus ticket, and we were on our way. It wasn't long before I realized that you take your problems with you wherever you go.

I was a hamster in a wheel running as fast as I could but never reaching a destination. Two short weeks, and in the end, Dave was ultimately right, and I had to go back and try to face some evident truths. Things wouldn't get better by ignoring the pain or moving away from everything that caused it. I realized that the town was fine. The people who lived in Narragansett were what made me miserable.

It was my poor decisions that had caged me in like an animal. It didn't matter if I moved down the street or to Alaska; I would bring my insecurities and problems with me unless I figured out how to change these obstacles into open doors.

Now, boarding for San Antonio, gate 5. Here I go. I hope Tracy is okay. I think of her every minute of my day and night. I miss her so much. Oh, my God, am I doing the right thing? It's too late now. Stop second-guessing yourself, Betty, I keep telling myself. I'm doing this for me and Tracy.

I grabbed my small bag and headed for the line. It would be another four hours before we landed at my final destination. I found my way to seat 20c and settled in. It wasn't long before we lifted off, and the Stewardess came by.

"Hello, I'm Sandra. Can I take your drink order?"

"Hi Sandra, yes. Can I please have some ginger ale?"

"We have peanuts."

"Thank you, that'll be great."

"Are you traveling for business or pleasure?"

"I'm not quite sure what you'd call it."

"Well, let me know if you need anything. Okay?"

"Yes, ma'am, thank you."

Sitting in my seat, I remember arriving back at Bob and Grace's after leaving Dave and Judy's.

I got a paper and found a couple of apartments and a job as a waitress. I looked up Joyce immediately to find out if we could share an apartment and save money. We may have grown up enough to live in the same house together.

Unfortunately, she was living back with her mother, trying to get her life straight.

I spent time with Margaret, catching up on each other's lives. I was amazed to find out what had happened since I had left.

She was pregnant and asked me what it was like having a baby around. Her parents had told her to keep a low profile in town, just as Bob did. Her traditional Italian background did not approve of her being pregnant out of wedlock, but her Catholic religion forbade abortion. She was a disappointment and had disgraced her family.

I felt sorry for her as she described the emotions of isolation and guilt. I could relate. I wished so much I could've said or done something to make her feel better.

She described how her wedding day was supposed to be, but things took a dreadful turn.

She said, "It was about 2 hours before the ceremony, and I was still getting ready when my mother ran up the stairs screaming. "He's dead, he's dead, oh my God." That's when she told me, Dean shot himself.

When the ambulance came, his mother was covered in his blood. I found out later, he called her into his room and put a sawed-off shotgun in his mouth and pulled the trigger.

"He killed himself on our wedding day when I was seven months pregnant."

"Do you know why he did it? Did he leave a note?"

"No note, no one ever knew exactly why except to say that his mother was very mean and controlling. She blamed me, saying I was a manipulating bitch that deliberately got pregnant to trap him into a relationship."

I could tell during our conversation that she was profoundly depressed and still devastated and not even close to being over the whole thing. I tried my best to keep her spirits up. We fell out of touch over the years but still send cards every Christmas.

I still worried about Joyce, so I also found time to spend with her. Sometimes, we hooked up with her other friends to spend time at the old Rocky Point Amusement Park. I met a nice guy named Glen. He was a tall, muscular, sandy-haired guy with a good job in construction. He reminded me of Dennis Leary. His gorgeous hazel eyes and slight overbite were highly sexy. The whole construction worker, bad boy façade turned me on.

Tracy and I lived on the second floor of an old three-story rock home from when she was three months old until shortly after she turned one. It had to be a 100-year-old home on Rose Court, just  across the street from Roxanne. It had a round tower on the ocean side of the building. I stripped all the paint off the wooden windows and repainted a peaceful blue ocean.

It had twelve-foot ceilings and green carpeted floors. The hallway and stairs have ornate old wood that represents the era of the house itself. Spring in the tower house was beautiful, and the scent of Honeysuckle and Lilac breezes filled the air. The view from the windows was astonishing. I could gaze through the trees of spring pinks and reds and the Yellow Forsythias in full bloom, right through to the clear blue sparkling ocean. I fell in love with this place.

I worked in Providence at ITT Grinnell, which is 30 minutes away.

Mom lost her license again, so she was only driving when she went to the bar. The drive was long enough for calming reflection, but I missed Tracy because I was away from home 10 hours a day. I had my place, a great boyfriend, and good friends surrounding me.

I introduced Roxanne to Linda, the girl upstairs, and we became tight friends.

Bizarre things started happening a few months after moving into the tower house. I felt strange sensations throughout the apartment.

One morning, I woke up to Tracy's wind-up swing clicking back and forth after it had run down the night before. Even though Tracy's crib was against the wall across from the foot of my bed, somehow, she ended up placed perfectly beneath it on the floor with her knees drawn up underneath her, having made no sound to get out.

Occasionally, I would wake up to my Pepsi bottle lids strategically placed on the floor, so I would step on them when I woke up. It was as if someone was playing childish practical jokes on me.

Accidents were prone to happen there as well. I'd never seen Tracy roll over before, so I wasn't worried when I turned for a second to grab some powder for her. I thought she was safe on the grooved bassinet, but she rolled over and landed on the tiled bathroom floor.

I turned to her screaming, scooped her up, and cuddled her while crying, "OH MY GOD, TRACY! OH MY GOD, ARE YOU okay, BABY? MOMMY'S SO SORRY, OH MY GOD, PLEASE BE okay!"

When we got to the ER, Tracy's head was very swollen, like a giant plum had grown under her skin.

I screamed at the nurses, "PLEASE, SOMEONE HELP MY BABY! SHE FELL ON THE FLOOR AND HAS A BIG LUMP ON HER HEAD!"

189

A doctor rushed in and took her from me, and I collapsed from the adrenaline rush to my head. After about an hour, the Doctor told us she was fine, but they still wanted to take some x-rays and keep her overnight just to be sure."

"I asked the Doctor, "Why do you need to keep her and do x-rays if she's fine?"

Roxanne was very supportive with her arm around me; as the Doctor explained, it was a good thing Tracy landed on the hardest part of her head because that's probably the only thing that saved her.

The Doctor told us, "She has a fractured skull, so she'll have to spend two days in the hospital; we just need to make sure her blood won't go into her brain."

For the next two days after work, I ran to the hospital and stayed with her until she fell asleep.

There was always part of me that wondered if something else helped her roll off that high changing table. She didn't roll over again for at least another month.

Our entity made it apparent that children were not welcome there. Although I ensured I childproofed the apartment, I was still afraid for Tracy daily.

I had to ask myself if this was a mischievous entity messing with my child out of jealousy or hate. I knew something wasn't right in the house; too many coincidences kept helping my child get into trouble.

I learned quickly to keep my eyes on her and look out for little surprises.

At 7 ½ months, Tracy was walking around holding onto the furniture, but by the time she was eight months old, she was walking independently and getting into everything. It seemed she had completely recovered from her fall.

Linda, my neighbor upstairs, was less fortunate with her three-year-old son, Leaves. She'd been arguing with her boyfriend for most of the morning. I could hear him tromping down the stairs as she called after him. He had every intention of leaving her. Linda locked Leaves in the apartment so he wouldn't be in the way.

As she argued with her boyfriend at the driver's side van window, she didn't notice Leaves somehow getting up to the lock, unlocking the door, and coming down the stairs. Unnoticed, he decided to play in the dirt. Just then, her boyfriend slammed his arms on the steering wheel before putting the van in reverse and peeling out of the driveway.

The van hit something, prompting him to stop. It turned out that the bump was Leave's head; he had wandered behind the back tire and was killed instantly under the crushing weight of the wheels.

His mother's reaction was horrific.

She screamed and did not stop until she lost her voice. Then she sobbed inconsolably day after day after day. The crying through the walls was never-ending. Sadness enveloped the Tower House; it hit all of us, but Linda was devastated...eating and sleeping were replaced by constant tears. Her mother took her to a mental hospital. I never saw her again.

That incident helped me realize how blessed I was to have Tracy in my life, and I needed to make sure she had a good life ahead of her. I realized I needed to keep Tracy close and protect her. I worried about leaving her with Grace.

I asked the owners about the history of Tower House. They said the family's small son drowned, and they couldn't bear to keep the house. His spirit might have lingered in the home because of the child's violent death.

Tracy and I were once again alone by Christmas. Glen and I fell apart because he could only hold a job for a month or two, and I couldn't afford to support him. I was lonely and often thought back to Daniel and wondered what Kurt was doing now. It's always during the lonely times when I think about my choices.

Although we were only briefly in the tower house, our landlord decided it was time for us to move again. He wanted to rent the house as a summer rental since it was so close to the beach, so he raised the rent so high that I couldn't afford it.

Part of me was relieved. I didn't want the vivid memories of Leaves to haunt me every time I looked out my window to the dirt driveway below. It was too much for me to keep replaying repeatedly in my head. I felt peace about leaving.

Shortly after Tracy turned one, we relocated into a single-story, 3-bedroom bungalow on Boone Street, just around the corner. I moved my friend Sherry, who was only 16 and thrown out of her mother's house, and her infant son Timothy  into the back bedroom to help them. By mid-January 1975, after only two months here, once again, our lives were changed forever.

It was the night of the Super Bowl; everyone had left, and it was cold enough in the house to turn on the wall furnace for the first time since I moved in. I awoke to billowing smoke wafting over my partitioned bedroom wall.

Instinctively, I ran to Tracy's room next to the fire. The heat in the living room was immense as the flames raged on, growing even closer to Tracy's bedroom. I had to move fast.

Tracy tended to climb out of her crib and wander around the house, so I pushed the couch in front of her door to protect her. By now, the sofa was on fire. I had to get her out of her room, so I sat on the floor and pushed the couch away with my feet.

With Tracy in my arms, I saw the fire cut off my escape through the kitchen and out the back door.

The only way out was the front door, and the fire was between us and the door. I screamed at the top of my lungs, "SHERRY GET OUT! GET OUT! THE HOUSE IS ON FIRE!"

I jumped over the flames towards the front door, which was bolted and locked. As I unlocked the front door, the hair on the back of my legs was singed. I was coughing, but I had to hurry because Tracy was exposed to more smoke because her room was closer to the fire.

We were burning up, and I couldn't get the latch off the screen door. We were going to die! I finally kicked down the screen door with one forceful blow and stumbled out of the house in my bikini undies and short top.

I stood on the street, clutching Tracy in her blanket and shaking from the cold.

Adrenaline surged as I screamed, "HELP US, PLEASE! HELP US, MY HOUSE IS BURNING. HELP US." Thank God there was a Super Bowl party across the street. The officer, Tommy Lanfere, who lived there, came out and took Tracy from my arms to check on her; my legs turned to jelly, and I thought I would collapse.

It felt like forever until the fire department came from around the corner. I sat there listening to all the destruction, my records popping,

193

smelling our belongings melting and being destroyed. Everything I owned was in that house, and when it was all over, all Tracy's baby pictures and cute dresses were gone, except for the photos Bob and Grace had.

All I had was gone, never to be seen again.

At only 18, I took one step forward and three steps back to their apartment again. Anyone else would've just given up by now, but I refused to give up. I was determined to prove my parents were wrong about me, but so much shit kept happening. Dad loved it when Tracy was around, but I knew my welcome would rapidly wear out, and I would have to get us out of there soon.

Chapter 20: Blood Strangers

Giving birth to Tracy amplified my desire to know more about my birth mother. Now that I was an adult, it was time I had some closure and visited her. But first, I needed a car. Since Tracy's birth, then the fire, Dad and I'd gotten much closer, and, in some ways, it was like old times again. When the three of us were together, the years of wear and tear from Grace's wild nights and ineptitude seemed to vanish. In Tracy, my once haggard dad had found his youth again.

When I scoped a Mustang for sale, Dad was almost more excited than I was. It was a steal at $150, which was all I had. We worked together to rivet new metal in the floorboards; the transmission needed a pressure plate, clutch plate, and flywheel; the tires were all flat and bald. The seats required covers, we stapled the headliner, and one of the headlights was busted. It would've made a great country song. Even so, to me, she was gorgeous.

I named her Bandit. She would be my ticket out of there as soon as Dad and I could get her together. We replaced the floorboards with sheet metal. He taught me how to drill holes and rivet them.

I had to replace the clutch plate, flywheel, and pressure plate in my transmission, and then we fixed everything cosmetically. Less than a month later, my chariot was ready for the trip to Illinois, and after 18 years, so was I.

I installed a CB radio to keep myself awake, talking to the truck drivers on the way. Between their chatter and grooving to my eight-track tapes of Elvis, The Beach Boys, The Beatles, and Roy Orbison, there was no time for dread. I was thrilled to be on the road and even more excited to meet Mary.

It seemed too good to be true.

Ironically, Grace was pissed. I'd never been anything more to her than a burden, yet when she had the chance to get rid of me, she didn't want it.

"Mom, I'm going to Illinois to meet my mother and the rest of my family."

"Yea?" she said with one arm over her eyes as she lay on the couch.

"Well, no matter what I do to improve my life, things just don't work out how they should. I try hard to be accepted by my family and friends, but I still feel like I don't belong here."

She took her arm off of her face and glared at me. "What do you mean?"

"I may have some roots to discover. I need to know who I am and why I don't fit in.

It could have something to do with my natural mother. It would be a good idea to go and meet her to get some questions answered.

"Questions? What's to know? She gave you up so she could keep her other kids. She would have asked you to come if she was interested in meeting you.

Why do you want to put yourself through that?"

"Well, we've been writing letters for some time now, and she said I could visit for a while to get to know her."

"She's just feeling guilty. You don't think she wants to have an extra mouth show up at her doorstep, do you? You're better off staying here and getting your life straight."

"If I stay here, I will never know the truth. I will spend the rest of

196

my life wondering what she's like. I need to take the risk for my sense of peace."

"I don't know why you need to become part of another family unless you feel like we aren't perfect parents."

"It's not that. You are the only parents I've ever known. I appreciate you taking me when she gave me up. I need to see her face when I ask her why she did it."

"Give it up, Betty. I know why you are leaving. You're running away from your problems again. Anytime you don't want to deal with a problem, you run away and go live somewhere else. Then you come back to us when you need someone to sweep up the pieces."

"I wasn't running away as much as running to a better life.

Can't you just be happy that I am trying to make sense of my life? If you love me like you say, let me move on?"

"We have always loved you! We took you when your mother couldn't keep you! If you loved us, you would stop running away all the time and making our lives miserable when we need to rescue you."

I knew she was right, but my pride wouldn't let me admit it. I didn't want to argue with her. I had to take a leap of faith; if I didn't, I would never know. Tracy and I decided to leave and make the trip without her blessings.

So, on a cool morning in May, one month after turning 19, while the dew was still on the ground, I put a mattress across the back seat of Bandit, and Tracy and I were on our way to Algonquin, Illinois. Along the way, I used the CB radio so much that the truckers dubbed me "Hot Lips." When they realized I was traveling with a child and that I was only nineteen, they took us under their wings.

A couple of times during our trip, Tracy and I rendezvoused with some truckers along the interstate who wanted to buy us dinner.

They were generous, friendly, and completely enamored with Tracy. I never once felt threatened, and I felt safer on the road than I ever did at home.

The truckers were a great distraction, but now and again, I'd think about how much of a risk I was taking. I was a single, unemployed teenage dropout mom. What would Mary's kids feel about me?

Just as I hit Algonquin, Bandit broke down for good. I called on the CB for help, and a tow truck hauled my baby away after all that work I did. The garage sold the car for parts. I had to laugh, or I would cry, thinking about how I would finally meet my mother by hitchhiking to her house.

I'd called Mary from the garage, so she was expecting me. When we pulled up to the little ranch-style house, I grabbed my backpack and Tracy and went to meet my birth mother.

Three younger kids came to meet me, but Ken and Kathy weren't there.

She had tears in her eyes as she took Tracy and hugged me.

"She doesn't look like anyone in our family, but she's still beautiful," said Mary.

The kids wrapped their arms tightly around Tracy and me. Thank you, I thought to myself. I'm home. Kenny was away in the service, and Kathy, only two years older than me, was working at the bank. As soon as she got home, she took me aside and said, "Don't think you're gonna be a part of this family; you will never be accepted here."

Kevin was 14, and Kyle, nine, was very accepting of us. Katelyn was only five, and she was a ball of energy.

I wanted to feel like I was contributing, so to help with some of the bills, I took a job at the Farr Company in Crystal Lake as an assembler. The work was monotonous, but factory work paid decently. After some long talks and a few months of trying to connect with Mary and her children, it finally hit me: I was never going to fit into their family. Sure, Mary and I had made similar bad choices; we'd both been teen moms and were keenly organized and strong-willed, but that's where the similarities ended. I crowded Mary, and she had her own life. And I had my own family, no matter how dysfunctional, and it was time I accepted it. Less than five months later, Tracy and I hopped on a train back to Rhode Island.

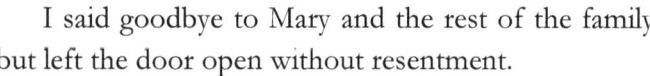 I said goodbye to Mary and the rest of the family but left the door open without resentment.

Even amid disorganization, growing up, I was always keenly organized. I was strong-willed and strived to be better than the mother that raised me. Grace was complacent and messy. I almost lost myself trying to be what everyone else thought I should be. I had no idea where to begin living because, although I had an instinct to survive, I had no guidance. Low self-esteem and insecurity dissolved somewhat once I stopped being a people pleaser and started using my God-given abilities to help others.

Part 4: Unsettling Changes

Chapter 21: Sink or Swim

Arriving back in Rhode Island, I looked at my parents in a new light.

Like it or not, Grace and Bob were in my life. I found comfort in finally accepting it, but that didn't lessen my desire to get out of their house. Luckily, I could find a winter rental in Point Judith almost immediately. It was a cute, off-season three-bedroom bungalow, so the price was right.

I had nothing in the way of furniture, so I went on a scavenger hunt. Dad bought me a small television and some kitchen stuff when we went to the flea market, but he couldn't afford furniture, so I got creative and reinvented myself.

I picked up some junk plywood, one-by-6s, and cinder blocks from a friend. He worked at a lumberyard. I made a couch from plywood and cinders and a bookshelf from the one by 6s and cinders. I sanded and used polyurethane to shine up two electrical wheels of different sizes and made my kitchen table and coffee table. I cut two barrels for my kitchen chairs and bought a beanbag for the living room. Mom took me to the fabric store, where we purchased batting and pillow material, and I used her sewing machine to put it all together. I got material for curtains as well.

I quickly found work as a housekeeper for a man who lived nearby. It gave me some flexibility to spend more hours with Tracy. It was not enough to make ends meet, so I got a roommate to stay in the front bedroom. The situation worked out nicely, but I still had to get a second job as a waitress in Point Judith.

Tracy was growing up so fast. As a baby, I could keep her from getting out of her room, but it became increasingly difficult to keep her out of trouble as she grew. There was not one ounce of patience in her tiny, curious little body, and she never slept!

I had Tracy tested at birth because her father took drugs, and I needed to ensure she had no permanent damage. The amniocentesis did not reveal anything abnormal. However, the brain wave test revealed almost two times more activity than an average child. The Doctor diagnosed her as clinically hyperactive and told me she would not need much sleep. That's an understatement. She slept an average of about four hours a night.

I woke up early one morning and thought it unusual that she was so quiet. She was painting a finger-painted mural on her bedroom wall. She created a masterpiece as high and as wide as she could reach. She thought she was quite the artist. The problem was that she didn't have any finger pain. She removed her cloth diaper and smeared the feces over the walls, creating what she thought was a beautiful picture. I was upset until I finally cleaned that stinky mess. Thinking back on it now, that was nothing compared to her next adventure.

The owners of the beach house made all the doors from woven bamboo.

When Tracy figured out, she could break through the door, there was no holding her back. One morning at 2 a.m., she decided she was hungry and proceeded into the kitchen for her goodies.

One of her favorite foods was peanut butter and jelly sandwiches, and she had watched me get it out of the top cabinets a thousand times before. It didn't take her long to figure out how to maneuver the kitchen chair to the counter and climb up. She pulled down the glass jars of peanut butter and jelly. After bouncing off the stove below, they crashed onto the floor into a thousand sticky pieces. How else was she going to get them open?

Then she sat in the middle of the glass with nothing on but a diaper. I woke to the smashing sound of the jars busting on the floor, but I wasn't sure what it could be until I saw Tracy's door chewed through.

Carefully, peeking around the kitchen corner, I found Tracy, smeared with peanut butter and jelly, sitting in broken glass, licking her fingers, and grinning ear to ear as if to say, "Mommy, look what I got!"

I was shocked, but at the same time, I was furious with her.

"Tracy! Stop! What are you doing? Get your fingers out of your mouth; that's broken glass!"

There was no time for shoes. Walking barefoot across the glass-ridden tile floor, I removed my baby from the debris and placed her in the tub. Amazingly, she didn't have one scratch on her, but I was not so lucky.

My feet were bleeding from three areas, though not bad enough for stitches.

Through all this, she was still my little helper. She loved to help Mommy vacuum and sweep. Sometimes, she rode on top of the vacuum cleaner, but if music played, she preferred dancing.

I was always devising different ways to keep her in one place, but she was always devising new ways to beat the system. At one point, I became so sleep-deprived that I almost fell asleep on my way to work. Tracy and I went on adventures everywhere together.

I loved her with all my heart but hungered for adult stimulation. At these times, I wondered what happened to Joyce. She'd dropped off the face of the Earth with her boyfriend, Lenny, and they were living in a trailer park.

203

Joyce came to Mom's house on the day I was there. She looked skinny, had bruises all over, and was pregnant. It was my first time seeing her on the verge of tears. However, Joyce never cried; I always thought that was strange until she told me it was because she learned not to cry when living with her mother.

There are times when a person should cry, and this was one of them, if for no other reason than to realize how hopeless your life is.

"Hi Joyce, are you okay? You don't look very good. Would you like me to make you something to eat?"

"No, maybe Lata. Right now, I want to rest. Can we talk lata?"

I took her into my room. After about three hours, she came stumbling out as if she'd just awoken from a coma.

"What is going on, Joyce? What happened? Where did you get all those bruises?"

She was overwhelmed by all my questions, but I was worried.

"I hate it thea in that traila with him. I cook, clean, and meet all his needs, but it's neva enough; he always finds a reason to hit me."

"You need to leave him; maybe you can stay at Mom and Dad's.

I'm living in Pt Judith, but I don't have any room in that little house."

"I don't know what I'm gonna do; I just need time to think. He can't even keep a job, and when he does wok, he doesn't make enough for food. He's high from when he comes home until we go to bed."

Joyce looked like a worn-out pack of bones with skin barely

hanging on her. Lenny displays his insecurities by beating on a weaker pregnant person who can't fight back, making him feel more powerful and in control.

Joyce was a victim of her childhood insecurities by believing she was not worth anything more than the beating she was getting. I felt so sorry for her and prayed that she would find the strength to pull herself out of the mire before she died.

When my lease was up in May, I moved to West Warwick, RI, into an old three-story New Englander on the third floor. The owner let it go. The paint was peeling off the walls, the kitchen counters were warped, and the shag carpet was matted. I hated coming home to the stench that thickened the air in that place.

Roaches scurried across the floor, and the mice ran rampant despite my attempts to fog them out. I wanted to prove I could make it alone, so I got an excellent waitressing job at the Showboat Restaurant within walking distance.

I enjoyed my job there, and I loved the people. It was here that I met Frankie Valley of The Four Seasons. I was waiting for a table on the other side of the big room when he noticed me and called me over. After a brief introduction, he told my boss I would be waiting at his table. He was cute but short and small-framed. Before they left, he invited me to a party, but I told him I had to get home to my daughter. Where's the camera when you need one?

My apartment was my first solo attempt since the fire, but the truth was I had to get Tracy out of there.

We both got sick often, and though Grace and Bob's house wasn't the most organized place, at least it wasn't physically hazardous to our health. Back to Bob and Grace's, I go. It's so frustrating not to be able to leave for good. I feel like such a failure, having lived in three states and 6 or 7 apartments to end up back here.

By the summer of 1976, I had successfully hooked up with Joyce.

We spent time together at Scarborough Beach, reminiscing about old times. I dropped Tracy off at Mom's because I knew we would be under the hot sun all day, and I didn't want her to get burned.

"So, you look much better; how have things been going since you left?

"She said. I finally got the nerve to leave him. I still caya for him, but I was afraid for Marlena."

Unfortunately, she was very lonely and more insecure than ever. I think she missed being with someone. I dated, but nothing serious; I never felt I needed a man. I didn't trust them yet, but I prayed that I might someday.

"Ya know, I take Tracy everywhere except work; she enjoys being with Mommy. How about you and Marlena? Do you take her with you everywhere?"

"I have no choice; I don't have anyone to help me like you. I don't have Grace."

"Well, I don't have her either. I keep Tracy with me because Grace still likes to drink, and I don't trust her."

She was back to her old snarky self and must've felt better. I wouldn't say I liked it when she tried to make me feel bad.

We were returning to the car when I spotted a man who looked like Babe getting ready to leave with his friend.

I prodded Joyce, "Hey, is that Babe?" I asked, pointing.

She looked to where I pointed and answered, "Yea, that's him."

"Wonder what he's doing here? His dad said he left the state."

Joyce jumped in front of me, "You need to tell him about Tracy."

"What do you mean? He probably doesn't even remember who I am."

"Betty, you gotta tell him about his daughta. It's wrong that he has a kid and doesn't know about her."

"Please. Babe couldn't give a shit about her, and he probably wouldn't believe me anyway."

"All I'm saying is that he should know. Just tell him, Betty. Do it now before he leaves. Come on. If you don't tell him now and he leaves, you might never see him again, and then you will always wonder what his reaction was. Just tell him now!"

I knew she was right, but I was still apprehensive about telling him. I inched up to him and tapped him on the shoulder.

"Hey, Babe," I said casually.

He turned around, and I could see his smile turn into a puzzled look. "Hello." He said with a furrowed brow.

"Do you remember me?" I inquired.

"No, should I?"

"You don't remember the times we spent together at the New York System, dinner at your sisters, or the night we were supposed to go out, but you took me to your house instead?"

He started to chuckle as if I were playing a joke on him.

"Betty?"

I got closer to him and lowered my voice. "So, you remember

having sex with me on your bed and then taking me home?"

Babe's face turned serious. "I'm sorry, but I thought you were into it."

"What gave you that idea? Was it the first, second, or third time I said no? You said you would call me back, and you never did. You used and threw me away after you got what you wanted."

"Listen, is this about revenge? Because I have a new life now, and I don't need to deal with old flames trying to get back at me."

"Really, well, I didn't even want to come over here and bother your perfect life, but my friend told me I needed to let you in on a secret."

"Yea, what's that?" he asked, smirking.

"You have a daughter," I said.

Babe stared blankly at me before snickering and yelling, "What are you talking about?"

"I'm serious. You have a daughter, Babe."

"Right. You probably had a kid with someone else, and you're trying to pin it on me."

"Look, I have no reason to drag you into her life.

I just thought you might want to know about her."

With that, the smirk was gone. I asked if he wanted to see my daughter.

"Yeah, I've got nothing to lose. Why not? How far is it?"

"About fifteen minutes from here."

"Okay, I'll follow you." He said.

Yeah, right, I thought, but sure enough, he followed us back to Grace's house, where Tracy was playing on the swing set.

She ran up to me, "Mommy, Mommy!" I swung her up into my arms and kissed her.

There was a moment of silence as Babe looked at her from his car.

"She looks just like you," I said.

His friend nudged him. "You should go check it out, man."

Joyce piped up and pointed at him, saying, "Hey, she's your kid; you can tell by looking at her that she's yours!"

Babe got out of the car, and his eyes got huge.

His buddy smacked him in the arm and said, "Hey, man, she looks just like you. Look at her! She looks more like you than her mother."

Babe sneered at him and rolled his eyes while I made a small crack of a smile. No one could deny that Babe was Tracy's father, especially not Babe.

"Look, I'm sorry I never called you back, and I'm sorry you had a kid. But the truth is that I'm engaged and having a baby with the woman I will marry. This can't happen right now. It would help if you hadn't waited so long to tell me.

"I tried to call you several times. Your dad said that you left the state and to stop calling. It wasn't my fault that you didn't get the messages. My intention was not to drag you into Tracy's life. We've been doing fine without you."

209

I paused momentarily, thinking of the harshness of my tone. "Would you at least like to talk with her?" I said calmly.

"I guess I could talk with her for a little while," he said, shrugging his shoulders.

He spent about ten minutes with her, and then he was gone. He didn't ask for a phone number or a picture. I couldn't expect much more than that. He had done the same thing to me. I knew then he would never be a part of her life, and you know what? I didn't want him even around her.

I was beginning to realize why I was so determined to have control over everything that happened in my life. The fear of being in the same place as before when I tried to take my life drove me to keep everything in check constantly. My life was hanging by a thread, and if I depended on anyone else to hold that thread, they would ultimately let go of it, and I would fall.

Now, I had two of us hanging by that string. I had trust issues and didn't think of anyone, but I could determine whether we failed or thrived.

I didn't have Joyce back in my life for very long. She decided she loved Lenny and would give him another chance. Back to the dungeon, being abused and lied to for the sake of not being lonely. I knew I had to continue my life, but I needed a better plan to make more money to support Tracy and me. In August of 1976, I found an opportunity to attend welding school. Welders got paid big bucks, and I knew we could make it on that money.

The Navy turned Quonset Point Naval base into a company called General Dynamics Corporation, Electric Boat Division. They started me out at ten an hour stick welding on high eighty-intensity steel in the bulkheads of nuclear submarines. Using various tools, I learned how to gouge metal and cut through steel plates. I was one of 2 women out of a crew of 15. Accepting women into a traditionally male role without a war going on was a brand-new concept. It was exciting to be a part of blazing a new trail.

Unfortunately, sexual harassment was commonplace for a woman to be belittled and degraded. Either you took it "like a man" or you "quit like a woman." Only whiners went to the supervisor to discuss harassment, and I was no whiner.

The work was hot and painful. We were learning to be structural welders who could weld in any direction, whether upside-down, sideways, or below us. Often, hot molten slag landed on me, making little burn holes in my clothes. I wore layered clothing under my leathers to avoid the smell and pain of burned flesh.

It was unbearably hot in the tanks. The sweat made my shirt stick like skin.

I used a denser lens in my welding shield than most because I burnt the corneas in my eyes. My headgear was too big for a woman's head, so I rolled up my bandanna and placed it under the band of my welding helmet until it fit snugly.

I'd been welding vertically overhead in a large tank all day, stopping only for a refill of oxygen when a chunk of molten steel, called "slag," dripped off into the top of my helmet. I could smell the burning flesh and hair, but as I was throwing everything down, getting my helmet off, and removing the bandana, the molten steel was burning through all the layers of skin. The bald spot finally filled in.

My welding experiences opened new doors on the relationship front. I met new people during my lunch breaks. Tim Mooney was a pipe welder working in the adjacent department. Of course, I had a bad habit of attracting the wrong guys, so I was cautious. I met Tim in the lunchroom. He wasn't tall or short; he was medium build and had short brown hair. He had a mustache and beautiful brown eyes. He was my intellectual equivalent, and we always seemed to have things to talk about.

I'd finally found someone who would respect me for who I was, and he got along great with Tracy. He always told me how impressed he was that I worked so hard and could keep up with the male welders. I never tired of his praise; I knew we could last if I wanted it bad enough.

Chapter 22: Submissive Warfare

Tim and I moved into the bottom floor of a two-story renovated home on Hendricks Street in Wakefield in February 1977. We'd been dating since October. Every day, I admired and loved him more. I was special to him, and he doted on me like never before.

Karen moved upstairs a few months before we arrived with her kids, Heather, Kate, and Jeremy. Karen wore beautiful, long, dark brown hair in a loose bun on the top of her head. Her tall, thin stature and smooth skin could have been model material, but her internal scars would never let her dream such a bold fantasy. She was from New York and used to be a nurse's aide, but she left the city to make a better, more relaxed life for herself and her kids.

She was divorced but somehow couldn't be free from her ex. I thought she had finally come to a point in her life where she could be at peace.

Like most of us, we carry many childhood demons into adulthood.

In her case, she had a spoiled Mother who found it difficult to show her any love.

Karen and I became close friends almost instantly. We drank hot tea in her house while I folded her laundry as we talked about our lives. Karen was great at entertaining and very smart but hated doing laundry.

Our children were only a year apart in age and got on great.

At three, Tracy had become more audacious and was testing my limits. I couldn't turn my back for a moment. She ran around naked, rebelling against any conformity.

She was responsible for putting her toys away and making sure her dirty things were in the hamper, and you would think this an easy chore, but for a strong-minded, stubborn child, this was not the case. I went into her room to tell her to pick up her things and stop jumping on the bed.

She yelled back, "Stop aggravating me."

"What did you say to me? Stop that."

"No, I don't want to."

"Tracy, get down off that bed right now."

"No."

I grabbed her and hauled her butt off the bed so fast she didn't know what hit her. She stood there in defiance with her fists on her hips and said, "No, I don't have to."

I tapped her on her bare butt and made her take a time-out. She, however, did not stop her death-defying behavior.

While having tea with Karen, I called for Tracy because the kids were too quiet. There was no answer, so I went into their room to find that Tracy had climbed out on the narrow ledge outside Heather Kate's 2nd-floor bedroom window. I almost had a heart attack. I could reach her arm and carefully ease her back into the window.

In August 1977, Tim and I married in a beautiful ceremony with the justice of the peace in our backyard among the lilacs. Karen was my maid of honor, and Tracy was our gorgeous little flower girl. Mom and Dad were there as well. And although Dad didn't seem quite himself, they felt relieved that I had finally settled down and wouldn't be moving back home soon.

After a while, Tim thought it would be a good idea for me to quit my job and stay home with Tracy. He told me I shouldn't have to work all those long hours, especially when he could more than afford our bills on his own. He said I could be with Tracy more often and volunteer at her preschool if I stayed home. I agreed to it. I was concerned that the housework was falling by the wayside. I couldn't stand a dirty, unorganized house.

It wasn't until I had a place and a real family to care for that I realized I had obsessive-compulsive disorder. I couldn't have any lint or dirty dishes in the house. I became a fanatic about every little thing being spotless. Every weekend, I would scour, polish, and disinfect every object in the house. Everything had a particular place. Our apartment was immaculate.

Was I overcompensating for the filth that I grew up in? Thanks to Grace, I realized I didn't want my home to be that filthy years ago. I remember what I did when I was pregnant with Tracy and lived at home. I would get on my hands and knees with a Brillo pad, Comet, and a razor blade to scrub and scrape the grease off the floors beneath the oil stove. I rubbed my knees raw, and my fingers bled. I was driving myself crazy cleaning, and Karen tried to help by getting me out of the house, but it wasn't enough. My new life of cleaning, caring for Tracy, and not working drove me into depression. No matter how much I tried to tell Tim, he didn't get it. He loved that his dinner was on the table every night, but that would soon be over.

Tim was fond of the bottle, but because of my experience with my parents, I forbid alcohol in the house. So, Tim got drunk before he came home from work. At first, I just went up to Karen's to avoid his critical and aggressive behavior, but I eventually had to go home, and that's when the interrogations started.

"What have you done all day, and who were you with?"

"I was upstairs at Karen's after I cleaned the house, helping her with her laundry."

"How come you didn't answer the phone when I called?"

"I didn't hear the phone; I was either upstairs or out in the backyard with Tracy."

It was one question after another, and if I didn't answer them fast enough, he cussed at me, calling me a Bitch, or made some degrading remark towards me.

He said, "What's wrong with you? Are you stupid?"

"You're wasting your time goofing off with Karen when you should be here."

He knew I couldn't stand the smell of whiskey and always expected sex after our fights. When I refused, he accused me of being a whore and cheating on him. His subtleness had turned into full-blown verbal abuse. There was just no way of pleasing him and his need for control.

At first, I thought he loved me so much that he was just jealous. How could a person change that drastically in such a short time? He often blamed me for our fights. I wanted the marriage to work out, so I believed him.

On his sober days, he loved to buy me gifts. He bought me new furniture for our home in October. I was at the height of my housecleaning compulsion, but the house never seemed clean.

Either Tim's constant attacks or Tracy's unrelenting curiosity was going to be the death of me.

One night, he agreed to go to Karen's party with me, and we had a good time. Then the party ended. When we entered our apartment, he pushed me against the wall and demanded sex.

Exhausted, I refused. "No, Tim, I'm exhausted; I had a long." I couldn't finish my sentence, and he slapped me to the ground and started accusing me, "You're having an affair, aren't you? Who is it?"

In his mind, I never wanted him because I was getting it from someone else.

I got up from the ground while he went into the bathroom.

Before he returned, I swiftly picked Tracy out of her bed and ran upstairs, locking Karen's door behind me.

He darted up after me in his stupor, almost falling down the stairs, and banged on the door.

"You open this door right now, Bitch, or I'm gonna kill you."

Of course, I feared he would probably kill me if I opened the door anyway, so I left it locked. To get my attention, he retrieved his shotgun and shot through the ceiling of our apartment into Karen's floor. Frantic, I called the police. Maybe they could calm Mr. Hyde back into my Dr. Jekyll.

When they finally arrived to get him, they had to break through our apartment door. Foolishly, I hurried down to make sure they wouldn't hurt him. I was too young to know that Tim deserved whatever the police wanted to do to him. Tim threatened them with a table leg, breaking off our end table. They were spraying mace into Tim's face and struggling to get handcuffs on him.

The police wrestled him to the ground as I said, "Please don't hurt him."

Tim's face was blood red as he said, "When I get out of jail, I'm going to kill you Bitch!"

"Do you want to press charges, Ma'am?" the officer said, trying to catch his breath.

I nodded my head no. I thought that if I said yes, he would follow through with his threat.

The police said, "He'll have to stay until he sobers up anyway."

I was grateful it was over. I wanted to believe that once the alcohol wore off, he would recognize the jerk he'd been. The following day, he was released. When his cab drove into the drive, I was standing at the sink thinking if I just kept my mouth shut, everything might go over smoothly. He barged into the house, grabbed my shoulder, twisted me around to his face, and shoved me back against the sink. Then he took his open hand and slapped me in the face with full force, knocking me against the wall.

"If you ever call the cops on me again, you will be very sorry, bitch! Do you understand what I have been through because of you? Why can't you do what you're told?" As I started to cry, he left for the shower, and I realized I was a prisoner in my own house.

Over the next week, Tim demanded, "You stop seeing Karen; she's a bad influence. Don't let me catch you up there again."

I believed it was because she advised me to stand up to him. Even Dad noticed the bruises on my arms sometimes and would stop by out of nowhere with a gallon of milk. He would say he was at the store and thought we might need some, but I knew he just wanted to check that everything was still okay with Tim and me.

November came, and it was time for Tracy's Birthday. I made her favorite chocolate cake and put it on the refrigerator for the next day.

Tim came home drunk once again, and we started fighting almost immediately.

I dreaded seeing him daily, but I had no choice; I was stuck here and had nowhere else to go.

He couldn't just go to take a shower like always; he had to end the fight by taking the cake and throwing it against the wall.

I made a new cake for Tracy at Mom and Dad's house and explained the situation to them. Of course, they didn't believe that he was to blame.

"Well, what are you doing to make him so mad at you?" Dad said.

"Nothing! I'm trying everything I possibly can to make this work. He won't stop drinking. It's the alcohol that makes him so mean."

Of course, they thought I was being trivial, and we went on with Tracy's Birthday party as planned.

Tim kept calling the house. Dad was getting upset and bullied me into dealing with it.

"You can't keep running away from him, you know."

"I'm not trying to run away. I don't want to be hit anymore. I want to be safe."

"You can stay here for the night, but you must go back home tomorrow, Betty."

"Okay, Dad," I said reluctantly.

Dad must have talked to Tim because things seemed to be going pretty well in our relationship for about two weeks, but I still couldn't trust him.

Chapter 23: Walk Softly

I needed peace of mind, someone to talk to who could give me the right advice. I picked up the phone and called my old Therapist, Mrs. Antonio.

She was surprised to get my phone call and was glad I trusted her enough to discuss my situation. She told me I needed a backup plan in case something drastic happened. She said men like that kill women and that I needed to be careful. One of the things she suggested to me was to go back and get my GED so that I could get a good job. I wasn't sure I had the confidence or knowledge to attempt such a thing, but I needed to try.

I made an appointment to get my GED in January, but while I waited, I studied.

Tim said, "You're not smart enough to get it without a tutor. You're an idiot for thinking you could just take the test."

I was determined and got a workbook so I could study and pass.

When the day finally came to take the test, I pushed everything negative aside and concentrated as much as possible. When it was over, I had no idea what the outcome would be, but I never regretted my decision to go. Dad was very proud of me as well.

TIM IMMEDIATELY CONFRONTED ME when I walked into the house and asked, "So, how did you do?"

"I have yet to find out; they said they'll send the results in two to four weeks.

"He said Well, I wouldn't hold my breath because you're too stupid to pass that test anyway."

I felt like I was back in junior high school when Martha called me names and beat me. Our marriage was on a roller coaster journey spiraling downwards.

Four weeks later, I received a passing score on my GED but couldn't openly celebrate.

I walked on eggshells in January but started feeling sick in February. I was in great pain one day and called Karen downstairs. When she arrived, I had doubled over in pain on the kitchen floor. Right away, she assumed Tim had beaten me. I was weak and dizzy when she took my pressure and pulse. The next thing I remember was going to the hospital and into surgery.

The Doctors found an ectopic pregnancy in my right tube, but luckily, they cleaned it before it ruptured.

Karen called Grace, who called Bob at work, but no one let Tim know. I was hospitalized for two days and released on bed rest with 25 staples in my lower uterus. Tim picked me up and took me home. He doted on me the first three days, then, one night after work, he came home drunk and pulled back the covers.

I woke scared to death, with flashes of the trauma from age fifteen. He smeared himself all over me, reeking of alcohol on his breath; I felt suffocated. I pushed him off onto the floor.

"What are you doing? You know what the doctor said? No sex for four to six weeks, at least until after I get these staples out." Then, I put my hand over my stomach to protect myself.

He grabbed my shoulders, demanding sex.

I said, "No, I can't; I have staples in my belly; I don't feel good. Please stop."

He screamed, "It's always something with you, you bitch.

Get up and act like a wife, I'm sick of your shit." Just then, he pulled me out of the bed and hit me in the belly. I doubled over in pain, grabbing my uterus.

"Oh my God, blood, I'm bleeding. What did you do?" Screaming as I pushed him down and started to run toward Tracy's room. I scooped her up with one arm as I held my insides together with the other. I left the door and ran down the road toward the Women's shelter on pure adrenalin with Tracy crying and confused, blood dripping from my belly.

"Help me, help me, someone please help me."

I heard him yelling and running after me as I turned the corner.

I banged on the door as hard as possible; a tall black guy in white scrubs answered the door just then. He looked behind me and saw Tim approaching the walkway, cussing and stumbling over himself.

I screamed, "He's after us, please open the door. He's gonna kill me."

He grabbed me and slammed the door in Tim's face. The orderly told him he was calling the police.

"That's my wife; you send her out here. Betty Lee, you get out here right now."

The orderly told him again, "The police are on their way. Go home."

"Yes, sir, we have an emergency. Some crazy guy is trying to kill his wife and pounding on the door. You need to come right now and send an ambulance. She's bleeding on the floor!"

The ambulance took me to the hospital, Tracy went to my parent's house, and Tim went to jail again. They stitched me back up and gave me fluids while I rested the next day.

Tim came to visit, trying to convince me not to press charges. He promised to attend AA meetings and be a doting husband. I felt sorry for him when he started apologizing to me yet again, but I knew he would never change. I was learning, though, and knew not to tell him that. Instead, I told him I forgave him, and everything would be okay.

The day I left the hospital, Karen picked me up while Tim was at work.

I told Karen, "I have to leave but don't know where to go. I can't function anymore. I feel like I'm just existing."

I was breathing, but Tim bruised my spirit. Someone called on the phone, and I would be incoherent. My daily routine was a blur. When it came time to feed Tracy, I would stare into the cabinets and try to figure out what I was doing there. I managed to take care of Tracy, but for the most part, I was roaming about in my own home, not understanding what purpose I had there.

Karen was my solace through this whole ordeal. I don't know what I would've done without her. She did her best to break through the confusion in my head.

I went to the apartment, got our stuff, dropped Tracy off with Grace, and left, telling her, "I can't, I just can't."

She said, "What? Where are you going?"

Finally, through prolonged efforts, her voice came through like a faint cry in the distant clouds of my mind. It was enough to hear the frantic alarm warn me about my desperate situation. I was able to come to my senses just enough to know I could not be a mom right now. Tracy needed someone to take care of her.

Ironically, Mom was the only person I knew who could take her. She was a better provider than I was right now.

"Mom, I need you to take care of her for a little while," I said, barely getting the words from my mouth.

"What do you mean? Where are you going? You're not just going to leave her here while you go out."

I looked at her tiredly, "Mom, please watch her for me.

I need to go."

"Go where?"

"I can't take care of her now."

"What are you talking about? Make some sense, Betty."

"I can't…. I can't." My arms flopped down, and I turned around to get into the car.

"Wait! How long are you going to leave her here?"

All I could say was, "I can't," repeatedly.

"Get back here! What do you mean you can't?" screamed Mom.

I got into the car and left her screaming at me with Tracy on the front porch, looking bewildered. I was utterly numb to feelings and started driving by instinct.

I remember driving up 95 North crying until my eyes blurred with uncontrollable tears. Through the fog, I saw the hospital in the distance, took the exit, and parked in the lot. I was in a daze as I walked through the front doors. I remember small bits and pieces of how I came to be at the door leading into the mental ward, crying.

I cried and slept for two days, and then, on day three, a therapist came in to talk with me. I told him what had been happening.

He said, "There are many cycles of abuse, and you may not recognize them while they're happening. You are strong-willed, so Tim had to win over your trust slowly. He got you to quit your job; that's the first step, and then he bought you a car and furniture to prove he was in charge.

"I didn't think anything of it. I thought he loved me and wanted to take care of me."

"He was gradually desensitizing you to verbal abuse and then, finally, physical abuse. You became comfortable trading your self-worth and independence for what you thought was a secure relationship."

"All I ever wanted was to leave my parent's house and love someone who would love me right back.

I've tried for a very long time to escape."

"When you dated, he got to know you well enough to know you needed that love and took advantage of your feelings.

You were submissive to him because you wanted to trust him. He, in turn, dominated you as if you were his slave. Your mother and father sealed the deal by blaming you for a failed marriage.

As a child of Alcoholics, it wasn't hard for you to accept the blame. You have been assuming responsibility for everything that's gone wrong in others' lives."

A few days later, I pulled myself together and decided that as soon as we could, Tracy and I were leaving. That was the last time I subjected myself to a beating by anyone.

225

I realized that the thought of my daughter and the love in my heart for her were the only things that drove my strength.

Tim attended two AA meetings and then realized I was never returning to him, so he stopped.

Sitting in court with my divorce lawyer, he told me, "Take it all; you can have it all. Take the new car and all the furniture."

"No, I don't want it. I don't want anything that reminds me of this awful experience."

"Sue him for alimony. You don't have a job because he made you quit. You need money to move into your place. Get alimony."

"No, I don't want anything from him. I need our clothes. I don't want any memories of him at all. I'm finished."

I left Tim for good in April 1978. This time, there was no separation; it was over. He wanted to stay the same for the right reasons.

Tim went to AA meetings because he didn't want me to leave, not because he admitted he had a drinking problem.

If people go to counseling to keep someone in their lives, their motivation comes from the wrong place. I didn't want my marriage to end. I did love Tim and tried to make it work, but at what cost? We'd been married for nine months. I was devastated to be divorced before our marriage began, but I was grateful to have gotten out before battered wife syndrome set in, and I had no hope and no will.

Chapter 24: I'm Sorry Daddy

By March 1978, my four-year-old and I lived back in my old room on Brown Street. Mom didn't want me to live with Tim, but she didn't care about me living at home either.

Since Tim had convinced me to quit my job, I had no money, and my welding certification had expired. I was stuck listening to my dad blame me for a failed marriage. Once again, all I could think was that another man ruined my life. I was walking on eggshells so Tracy and I wouldn't be out on the street.

I took Dad aside one night and asked him for some advice, thinking that would be an excellent way to get him to open up to me again.

"Dad, I've been thinking of my situation and how to start my life over. I have some options, but I've been considering joining the military.

What do you think?"

He looked at me as he spoke, saying, "Well, you have your GED now. Tracy would have all of her medical and dental bills paid.

You would never have to worry about a place to live. I think it's a good idea, but do you think you're disciplined enough to take orders?"

"I'm willing to try. Is it a good idea, Dad?

I mean, I don't have any place to put Tracy while I am in basic training."

"We can work it out, Punkin. You remember two things. When you join the military, stay in for life. Second, follow orders so you don't ask why or how, even if they tell you to get a bucket of steam. You do it."

Dad and I were talking again. We had a long conversation about my options, but I thought the military would be the best for us. The only thing I could get out of the discussion was to stay in for life and do whatever they told me. He was an old Navy lifer guy giving tough advice to his daughter. I loved my dad and knew he would somehow always be there for me, just as he was when I was a little girl. Sometimes, you only know when to cherish conversations with someone once they're gone.

On Memorial Day weekend, May 26, 1978, Dad asked me to clean up the barbeque grill so we could cook out the weekend.

"Of course, great! I'm so glad we're finally getting a chance to have some fun. It's gonna be great, Dad. Do you want me to cook anything else for the cookout? What do you think about some potato salad or beans?"

"Yeah, why don't you make something up tomorrow, and we'll cook out in the afternoon after I wake up."

"I can't wait," I said.

We talked briefly, and then he got ready to work that night. He said he was taking the weekend off. That was unusual since he'd been working seven days a week for as long as I could remember. Dad was in such a good mood; I thought now would be a good time to discuss exchanging bedrooms.

Tracy and I stayed in a ten-by-ten room with my dresser and two beds. I didn't even have a closet, and I tripped over everything.

I asked Dad, "Would you consider switching rooms with us temporarily until I figure out what I will do."

He snapped back and said, "This is just a temporary situation, and you have no business asking me for my room because this is my house.

We both said some choice words while we argued back and forth, bellowing at one another. I was so mad at Dad for being so selfish that I blurted out, "I'd rather have a dead father than a father like you."

I slammed the door to my room and came out after he left for work. I didn't say goodbye.

My cat, Tinkerbell, made me realize something strange was about to happen.

Our cat Tinkerbell regularly went to Dad's bed whenever he left for work. Still, this time, about 45 minutes after Dad left the house, she went to his doorway and sat there patiently, looking up at me as if she were waiting for permission to enter the bedroom.

I leaned down to her and asked, "What's the matter, Tink?"

She peered back at me with glowing green eyes, still sitting on the threshold of his door, and then turned around to fixate on the bed. I stared into his room at the unmade bed to see what she was looking at. There was an eerie silence in the house.

After about 30 minutes, the phone rang. I jumped. I picked up the phone to an unfamiliar voice.

"Mrs. Ott?"

"No, she's not here right now. Can I help you? This is her daughter?"

"I need to speak to Mrs. Ott."

"She went out and won't be back for a while. I am her daughter; can I help you?"

"Ma'am, there has been an accident."

"What do you mean? Who had an accident?"

"It's your father."

"My father? Is he okay? What happened?"

"Well, we need you and your mother to come to the emergency room at South County Hospital."

"Is my father okay?"

"It's complicated, ma'am. We need you to come down."

"Okay, I'll get my mother, and we'll be right there!"

I called Gail across the street to watch Tracy until we got back. She said, "No problem. Bring her right over."

Mom already had a couple of drinks when I drove down to Terminassi's, so leaving wasn't an emergency. I screeched into the ER parking area and ran to the front desk.

"Do you have a Robert Ott here?"

The lady hesitated for a moment and started fumbling for words.

I asked again, "Is my father here? His name is Robert Ott."

Mom came through the glass doors and to the desk to ask about Dad. The nurse stepped from behind the desk calmly.

She called us over to the side of the desk, pointed just to her right, behind her desk, and said, "Go around here and to the right."

I looked around, and to my left, I couldn't see anything.

When I looked to the right, I saw a gurney with someone moving under a white sheet with a big belly. I couldn't see that person's head at the other end of the gurney.

I walked up hesitantly, saying, "Dad… Dad, is that you?

Hey Dad, are you okay?"

When I got there, it was a different man. I said, "I… I'm sorry--I thought you were my dad."

He didn't say anything. Mom was standing in the doorway of the hall entrance, looking at me.

A doctor came out of the room to the right, just beyond the gurney, and said, "Miss Ott? Then, he looked at Mom and said, "Are you Mrs. Ott?

Mom said, "Yes, what happened?

Where's my husband?"

I asked, "Where's my dad? I got a call saying there was an accident. Can I see my dad?"

I looked past the doctor standing in the doorway of the small room to another gurney with a body on it.

"Is that my dad? Hey Dad, are you okay? What happened?" I yelled, standing on my tip toes to see past the doctor.

The doctor reached out and held my forearms. I instinctively pulled away.

I said, "What are you doing? Let me see my dad! Dad!

Dad!!"

The doctor said, "Honey, I'm sorry. We did everything possible to save him, but he died on his way to the hospital. He…."

"You have no idea what you're talking about. My Dad didn't die."

"Miss, your father died from a heart attack. The ambulance arrived too late and couldn't give your father CPR. They couldn't revive him because they couldn't massage his heart."

"No…" I said, fading off.

I slumped against the wall and fell into a void of nothingness like a soundproof bubble. The doctor's lips moved slowly, but no sound came out.

I felt such a deep pain in my chest that I couldn't breathe or talk. It was as if someone had stopped time, and I was the only one there. *I'm sorry there was an accident.* Those words played over and over in my head.

I don't know how Mom took the news because I was in my world. When I returned to reality, I asked, "Can I see my dad?"

The intern said, "Yes, Ma'am, he's in here." He led me into another room.

They had put a white sheet over him. Walking over to him, I was still crying and unsure I wanted to see Dad.

"Ma'am, are you ready? Do you need to take more time?"

I stood there for a few minutes before I nodded yes. Dad looked so peaceful, as if he was sleeping; it had been a long time since he was not in pain.

Mom did what she knew best to cope with our loss.

Immediately after the news, she turned to the whiskey bottle, getting drunk and crying. I was beyond distraught and disheartened, walking into a nightmare I couldn't wake up from. I felt confused and didn't remember how I got home. To this day, that day was a blur of sadness.

I went to the only person I thought would understand about Dad's death. I BROKE DOWN AGAIN when I got to Ginny's house and told them all the solemn news.

Ginny took me in her arms while crying for the first time. She told me to be strong and that I would get through it.

The following day, Ginny told Mom about Forbes Funeral Home in Wakefield. That was where Ginny went when her husband and baby died. She called Mr. Forbes to set up an appointment for the next day. I went with her, but Ginny interjected herself into the arrangements. Mr. Forbes asked about the insurance, what kind of casket he should have, what he would wear, and the flowers. It was so surreal.

That night, Mom got drunk again; I took her to the funeral home in the morning. Mom told Mr. Forbes she would get $10,000.00 from his work and monthly widow's benefits from his time in the Navy.

She said, "He was a veteran, so I'd like him buried at the Veteran's Cemetery in Exeter. Is that possible?"

Mr. Forbes gave Mom some numbers to call and said, "Here are the numbers you'll need to arrange for the burial and to check on the rest of your benefits."

Retirees leave their wives with widow's benefits. They're usually not much, but they're more than Social Security, and they increase every year. Dad was making payments for these benefits every month.

Mom turned pale when the military informed her that Dad canceled his widow's benefits just a few months before his death. Dad had a mild stroke, but only Tim knew, and he made him promise not to tell anyone. He was only 51 years old; why would he not try to help himself, if not for him, but for us? Tracy will never get to know her grandfather.

Grace picked out the most expensive gray metal casket they had. She told Mr. Forbes to bury him in his Navy dress whites with all his metals; then she ordered three hundred dollars of flowers. She gave Ginny two hundred dollars for the food and the wake and invited all her bar friends to both. In the meantime, I called the Navy, pretending to be her, to arrange the military funeral and called the Social Security office to find out about Dad's Social Security benefits.

I tried to help her as much as possible with the arrangements, but every time I talked about it, she said it was none of my business.

"Stay out of this!" she snapped at me.

She got in my face and pointed her finger at me cruelly.

"He's dead because of you; this is your fault for being so stingy; you just had to have your way! You couldn't leave well enough alone! Well, now you have his bedroom, don't you?"

"What? Are you crazy? This had nothing to do with me!" I said in total disbelief.

"Don't give me that. If you didn't have that argument with him the other night, he would still be alive. You caused this!"

She started crying, turned around, and left me standing there.

Tears in my eyes, I was stunned.

I knew I didn't cause his death, but after playing her words repeatedly in my head, I started to believe them.

Maybe it was my fault. How could I be so selfish, so self-centered as not to consider Dad's feelings? Why did I have to open the subject? I wasn't planning on staying there anyway.

Why couldn't I leave it be?

Knowing he died because I broke his heart, I had to live with that for the rest of my life. I disappointed him. I asked too much of him. In the end…I killed my dad, my best friend, and my mentor.

I couldn't face being in the wake, especially after she said what she had done in front of Ginny. I knew I would fall apart. I only wanted to remember how he used to be anyway, not as a lifeless body.

On the day of the wake, Forbes invited the family to come and view Dad before everyone else got there.

Joyce, Marlena, her daughter, and Susan came down to help me with Tracy and help Mom with the arrangements. Mom had on her brightest lipstick, and I was barely hanging on emotionally. My eyes were red and swollen from tears. My head was pounding from crying so much. I wondered how I could have any left at this point.

On our way up the stairs to Forbes Funeral Home, Ginny pulled me aside as Joyce went ahead with Tracy.

"Why don't you just straighten out? What the hell is going on with you? Don't you see how much you're upsetting your mother? It's already been two days, and you're acting like a child."

"But Ginny, I can't… I don't know what to do. I miss him so much; I can't stop crying."

"That's enough! You don't enter that room until you can compose yourself and stop all that blubbering. You're being selfish; get a hold of yourself. Do you understand me?"

She had just told me I wasn't allowed to feel any remorse for my dad's passing. My heart broke now that my dad was gone, but the hurt towards a woman who spent her life beating me down proved I still had one.

I composed myself enough to sit in the back of the room.

Roxanne, Margaret, and Debbie sat by the front with their families. Karen came back to sit with me and Joyce. The funeral director motioned for me to sign the book, but I held one hand in front of my nodded head and declined politely. Ginny's eyes darted back to me, and she sternly took her pointer finger and commanded me to take my place beside her, Mom, and Susan.

With my head down, I walked up to the front and sat hesitantly in my seat. Ginny's eyes burned through me before she finally looked away toward the casket. She was treating me like some rebellious teenager who was deliberately seeking the attention of others. I just wanted to hide from everyone. I didn't even want to be there.

When everyone started to get up to see Dad, I took Tracy and declined again because I knew I would start crying again.

Ginny came up to me and said, "Come on. It's your turn. Let's go."

"Please, Ginny. I don't want to go right now. It hurts too much."

"What? I can't believe you are still thinking of yourself. Your mother must suffer through all this and be strong while looking at her dead husband; I swear, Betty Lee, you can be so self-centered."

Ginny knew that Mom had to have a few drinks before she came here. I was sober.

When everyone had sat down, I gave Tracy to Susan and crept up to the casket. Tears gently and quietly rolled down my cheeks as I attempted futile reconciliation with him. He didn't even look like my father now. His skin had an eerie orange tint, and he was so dry. "Daddy, I'm so sorry," I said, crying uncontrollably. I miss you so much. I'm so sorry for what I said."

I bent down and kissed him on his cold cheek. Just then, Ginny came up behind me and grabbed my shoulders.

"That's enough; you're making a scene and upsetting your mother. Let's go.

I yanked myself away from her and sobbed more freely.

"No! You leave me the hell alone! Don't touch me!" I turned back to my dad and started speaking a little louder.

"I'm sorry, Daddy. I love you, and I miss you so much." I turned and left the room, blinded by my tears. I grabbed Tracy and left.

Ginny, Mom, Susan, and Joyce met us in the car, and on our way home, Ginny took another opportunity to embarrass me by warning me.

"We'll be going to the evening wake. I hope you don't think you will act this way then. Try to straighten yourself out before tonight."

I had so many emotions running through my head that I thought I would snap. I had to get myself under control. I was grateful that Joyce was there. She took care of Tracy and provided a shoulder.

"Betty, ignore Ginny; she's just a Bitch.

You know she always wants to be in charge. Just ignore her."

"She's always hated me, and now she has a chance to manipulate and embarrass me. I think she's enjoying this."

"I've always hated Ginny," Joyce said, trying to comfort me.

"She's mean; always mean to us and her kids."

Joyce and I have never been very loving toward each other, so, unfortunately, I never got the hug I needed.

Joyce said, "Why don't you try to get some sleep? You look exhausted; get some rest."

I fell asleep on my bed while Joyce took Tracy to the other room with Mom and Susan.

Dad died on a Friday, and Monday was Memorial Day, so his wake was two days long. I had two days to look at him and remind myself how selfish I was about something so trivial.

Everyone I had grown up with had turned to drugs, alcohol, or abusive relationships, and I had to find a way out.

Dad died, Mom jumped headfirst into the whiskey bottle, and I had come to hate her for it. Work was scarce, and I had a four-year-old to support.

We buried Dad on Tuesday morning in the Veteran's Cemetery with full Military honors. He was glorified more by leaving the earth than living on it. My father was a man who never owned his own home or knew what it was like to experience the smell of a brand-new car. He had no expectations of pleasure in this world and left not one bill to pay.

He always said, "If you don't have the money to buy it, you don't need it."

He was a simple, generous man with simple needs: no frills, no new clothes, and no delusions of what his future would bring.

He worked every day, for that day, and the next. Finally, Dad knew what peace was.

"Ma'am, are you okay? Sandra, the flight attendant, asked. "I'm fine; I'm just not sure of my choices. I don't know if this is where I should be."

Chapter 25: Too Afraid to Stay

A few weeks later, I awoke to Ginny's voice in the kitchen. She and Mom were at the kitchen table talking about how Mom would spend Dad's insurance money. She was insulted that dad canceled his widow's benefits, which meant she couldn't afford basic living expenses. Two weeks had barely passed, and she couldn't get through one day without a drink. Susan had returned to the city, but Joyce stayed in my room to help me with Tracy. She was a godsend for me during this time.

I was so sick of looking at Mom and Ginny day after day.

I asked Joyce to watch Tracy, and I jumped in the Nova and drove to the Ace of Clubs, about forty minutes away. Any dark corner in the back of the room would do, as long as I got away from the pity party for a while. It was lunchtime when I walked into the empty bar-empty except for the guy standing over at the counter talking to the two owners, Bobbi and Junior. The Ace of Clubs was a husband-and-wife establishment.

They knew my parents well because, time after time, they saw me peel Mom from the bar stool and drive her home.

I sat there hugging a Seven-Up, pondering my escape. Tim was continually bugging me to return to him, believing I was weak enough to give in, and Mom was nudging me in the same direction to get rid of me. Of course, when I told him no, he was furious and trying to manipulate me, but I could see right through him.

Pushed way back into the depths of my mind, thoughts of the military hovered just out of reach. *Was I good enough? Was I strong enough? How could I leave with all the unfinished business here at home? Who would take care of Mom? I would have to find foster care for Tracy if I went, but*

240

I couldn't stay here with all the drama. How would I teach my child she could be anything she wanted to be? I hadn't accomplished anything to be proud of.

From the back table, out of the corner of my eye, I caught the stranger pointing at me.

"Who's that?" I saw him ask.

"Oh, that's Bob and Grace's daughter, Betty Lee," said Bobbi.

"Who?"

"They were frequenting here, usually at night," said Junior.

"What's she drinking?"

"Seven-Up," said Bobbi.

He looked at me and said, "Well, let me have another one for her."

"You gonna go talk to her, Mike?" said Junior, handing him the soda.

"Yeah, she looks lonely."

Bobbi said, "Yeah, she just lost her dad; he was such a great guy."

He made his way over to me and set the glass of soda by my almost empty drink. I looked up at him through stinging, blurry tears.

"What's that for?" I said timidly.

"It's for you."

I looked back down into the clear sparkling soda.

"Thanks. Who are you?"

I asked.

"My name is Mike. Are you okay? I'm sorry about your father. Is there anything I can do?"

"I've never seen you here before. Are you from around here?" I inquired.

"Yes, I live in Exeter. We may not come here at the same time. I come here for lunch on my break."

"Lunch break? What do you do?"

"I have my own business. Mostly, I install pools for people in the summer and sell cords of wood in the winter. I set my prices and my hours. It's a living."

The guy was nice, but I didn't feel like talking.

"Listen, I hope you don't mind, but I'm not in the right frame to talk to anyone right now."

"I can see that you're very upset. Is there something I can do to help you?"

"You don't want to be with me right now. I'm in a crisis here and won't be pleasant to be around."

"I understand, but I'm a good listener, and you look like you could use a friend."

"Thank you, Mike; you're right; it's been so hard to face the reality of never seeing my dad again, and no one seems to care about my feelings."

Over the next hour, I couldn't help but notice how muscular he was in those coveralls with his beautiful, tanned body. I gave Mike a short overview of recent events, starting with my daughter Tracy, Tim's abuse, my pending divorce, my father's death, and my decision about the military. I could see in his eyes that he was overwhelmed. I felt terrible unloading, but it felt great to get it out. I felt at ease with him.

"I see," said Mike, taking a deep breath.

"So here I am drowning my life in a glass of Seven-Up because I would never give my mother the satisfaction of knowing she drove me to drink."

"Wow, that bad, huh?"

"I told you. It's not a good time for me."

"Alright, you're having a tough time getting on your feet.

Things have to get better from here," he said, smiling.

"You don't understand. I have been waiting all my life for things to get better. The more I think about it, the more I realize there is nothing for me here. I can't get away from this place! It's like a black hole." I said, looking down at my drink.

"Maybe you need to meet the right person. Maybe it's not the town, but the people in your life."

I looked at him with cynical disbelief. "You don't say."

"Sorry. I didn't mean to make it seem so minor."

"No, I'm sorry. Forgive me for being so sarcastic about it. I need a change of scenery. Every time I leave this place, I end up coming back. This place is all that I know. I've been surrounded by white trash my whole life. I don't want that for Tracy. I know that I don't belong here."

"Where do you think you belong? Where do you want to be?"

I sighed. "I don't know. There has got to be something else out there. I don't want Tracy to learn to live on welfare. I want her to have a future, some hope, you know?"

I looked up and stared into his beautiful and intoxicating crystal-cool blue eyes. I opened my mouth to speak, but he interrupted me.

"Do you have any plans for tomorrow?"

"No, I'm probably just going to sleep. I've been doing a lot of that lately."

"How about I take you out somewhere away from all that," he said, smiling.

"No, I don't think so. I'm just going to stay home tomorrow. I wouldn't be very good company."

Mike got closer to my face, "You're here, aren't you?"

"I came to sort out my thoughts…*alone*," I said, looking away.

"Look, you can't stay home tomorrow. You should get out and try to live. I'm not asking you to sleep with me. I want to take you to breakfast, no strings."

"I don't know, I'm kind of emotionally strung out right now." I reached for the napkin and began twisting it. *It would be nice to have an excuse to get away from Grace.*

"So, get away from the drama for a little while. He said, reading my mind. Let me take you and Tracy to breakfast; then you can see what I do for a living."

Wow, he included Tracy. That's a first.

"You want both of us to come with you to work?"

"Why not? The boss won't mind," he said, winking at me.

I smiled and looked up at him. "Okay, why not? I *do* need to get out of the house. I'll give you my number, and you can call me tonight."

He took the napkin and said, "I'll talk to you later tonight then. Please feel better."

Joyce was staying at Grace's with me, so that night, I asked her if she knew about Mike, and it turns out she knew him through her ex-Lenny.

I asked, "Well, what kind of man is he? How well do you know him?"

"I've known him and his brother for a couple of years. They're nice guys; they live in Exeter."

"So, you met him through Lenny?"

"Yeah, but they weren't together at the bar; they just knew each other."

"So, what does Mike do? Does he work?"

"He works for himself doing odd jobs, he sells wood and fixes cars, and I heard he helped build a house."

"He's got lots of talent and very cute, too."

"I always thought he was."

"Oh, and he does landscape in the summer."

"Really! Is there anything he doesn't know how to do?"

"I'm not sure."

"I was only kidding. I'll get to know Mike better, and he invited us to breakfast.

"Who's us?"

"Me and Tracy"

"He invited Tracy?"

"Yup, weird. Hah?"

Mike and I talked daily and spent as much time together as possible over the next two months. I never hid the fact that I had to get out of there. He knew I was serious but never stopped convincing me I should stay.

Ginny talked Mom into giving all dad's things to the Barbers and the Brindamours. The bunk bed Dad had put together for me went to Ginny's children. The Brindamour boys got Dad's hunting rifles and clothing, some still strong with Dad's familiar scent. Joyce got away with my brass bed and some of Dad's favorite trinkets, including the shaving brush and cup I used to watch him shave with. I had wanted Dad's shaving cup and brush, but Grace swooped in before I could grab it.

They cleared everything out and left me without any indication of my father's presence in the house. I snatched his wallet and a pipe stand, which I quickly hid away along with his memory concealed deep within my heart.

I felt I never existed in his world when she gave Dad's stuff away. She turned her back on me.

I spent all those years yearning to be a part of the family, to experience the brunt of their neglect while they pursued their interests. The only parent who reached out to hug me or try to be there for me was gone, and I wasn't entitled to any of "His" things that conjured up fond memories of him. Even in grief, Grace could be so cruel.

It was the beginning of August, and I couldn't sleep thinking about Mike and how much I loved him. How could I leave him? But I can't stay, or my soul would die.

The following day, Mike pulled up in his big yellow, bondo-ridden truck, his thick, dark, wavy mane barely moving as the wind blew through the open window. Spending time with him was no trouble at all.

I hesitated to talk about leaving again, but I also had to find out where Mike was coming from.

"I hardly slept last night, which is why I look like this," I explained.

"Why? Are you upset about something?"

"I had my mind all set and was looking forward to getting away from here, then you happened. You came into my life, and I'm confused."

"So, does that mean you're staying?"

"My head is saying LEAVE, get out! My heart is saying, stay. I honestly don't know right now."

"And you stayed awake all night thinking about it?"

"Well, yes, but only because of you."

"What do you mean?"

"I love you, so it's not an easy decision." I blurted out.

"I love you too, Betty; let me be your future. I'll build you a beautiful log cabin in the woods and care for you and Tracy. I promise I will work hard to give you your dreams. You don't have to leave, Betty. Let me show you that not all men are monsters. I love you and will always provide for you and Tracy."

I love you. Though it was the first time Mike had said those words to me. I found myself analyzing the true meaning of love. Being abandoned, tossed around, beaten down, and belittled didn't give me a solid idea of what love was.

My thoughts immediately went to Tim, who had promised to take care of me just one short year ago. *Was he luring me in so he could control me? No thanks! But what if he wasn't? What if he's the one?*

"Mike, last night I looked back on my life and realized I don't know who I am, I don't know who to trust, and I have lots of issues to clear out of my life."

"Can't you figure all that out here?"

"I would love nothing better; you know how much I love you, but I've had a plan since before Dad died. I discussed it with him a few weeks before, and I feel good about it."

I found myself thinking about all he had to offer. He was quite a catch. He's a mechanic, auto body repairman, pool installer, house builder, and jack of all trades. He was a freelancer who lived by the laws of his land, an independent. He was just the kind of man I needed.

What am I thinking? This kind of thinking keeps getting me into trouble.... *My situation wouldn't ever change unless I changed it. What was I waiting for?*

The following month, we got to know each other very well. Mike took to Tracy like a fish to water. Very rarely did he ever suggest a babysitter for her. We went everywhere with him. I was in love for the first time, and it felt good. So why did I hesitate? It all comes down to trust.

So many people in my life have said one thing and done another. I didn't trust what people said and was tired of being manipulated and hurt.

I had no sense of responsibility for Grace, so why was I still here? There was nothing for me here except Mike, and I wanted to trust him, but something inside me told me I couldn't depend on another man for my happiness.

I had run to another Prince Charming only to find the beast behind the mask. I'd had enough of guys saving me. Where did it get me? Nowhere!

They were like my drug of choice.

Their soft words and sexy bodies were just a drug to numb reality.

I realized that individuals could go through their lives under the impression that they are a particular person. However, there is a time when we come to a crossroads, and we must leave childhood expectations behind and make our future.

Chapter 26: Survival Trumps Fear

Mike and I sat in front of Grace's house. I was on one side of the seat, and he was on the other, which was very unsettling. I loved to cuddle up close while he drove, but tonight was different. I wasn't giving him any misconceptions that I was staying and didn't want to make it more difficult on me simultaneously.

We talked about staying together after I came out of basic training, and I told him," If you still feel the same way...Yes, I would love that." Noticing his frustration, I spoke up again to reassure him,

"Mike, this is a good thing, you'll see. I can support Tracy, and we'll have benefits and a place to live."

He turned away and looked straight ahead. Then he put the truck in gear and started to drive.

"It sounds like you've already made up your mind. The military is not my idea of stability.

I couldn't live with someone telling me what to do every day. I wanted to get to know you and Tracy better.

"We can write while I'm training; I'd love to get your letters."

"I don't write well. So, what will you do with Tracy while you are in training? You can't take her *with* you, Betty."

"No, I know, that's my catch twenty-two. If I don't go, neither of us may have a future. If I do go, I'll have to leave Tracy with Mom, and in her condition, it will be a miracle if Tracy survives basic training. Even if she can get through raising Tracy alone, Mom will still ruin her emotionally. She doesn't have a clue how to raise a child. Aside from having Tracy, this is the most challenging decision I have ever made.

I have to make it alone for a little while. Please try to understand. I can only continue to rely on myself for my needs. I gotta know what kind of Woman I can become alone."

"I understand and know what you mean about making it yourself first. Have you talked to a recruiter yet?" he asked, turning into the diner."

"No, but I will very soon.

I need to check out my options. I thought about going into the Navy like Dad, but I didn't want to be away from Tracy for so long. I couldn't even think about going into the Army or the Marines; I don't think I'm strong enough."

"Well, what else is there?

What about the Coast Guard?"

"No, I was thinking about the Air Force. I want to talk to an Air Force recruiter. I hope I can get in. I didn't graduate, I had to get my GED, and then there's the whole single-parent thing I have against me."

"You won't know what will happen until you ask. I wish you luck…I do, even though I want you to stay."

Mike dropped us off and went to work.

The following day, I called the Air Force recruiter.

"Hello, Sir; I wanted to ask you some questions about joining the military."

251

"Yes, Ma'am, I would happily help you with those questions."

" I wanted to enter the Air Force, but I am getting divorced and having a child."

"Do you have custody of your child, Ma'am?"

"Yes."

"Good, basic training is seven weeks long. Do you have someone to watch the child while you are gone?"

"Yes."

I didn't know where she would stay, but I knew I'd figure something out.

"Now, do you have a high school diploma?"

"Unfortunately, I dropped out, but I did get my GED. Can I still get in?"

The gentleman paused for a moment.

"Have you considered why you want to join the military, Ma'am?"

"I want a better future for my daughter and me. I believe the military will help me achieve that."

"I see. Well, I can tell you this. The Air Force has been strict about these two things in the past. However, our government has relaxed its criteria over the last two years. I'm not sure how much longer we will be accepting single parents with GEDs, but for this moment, we are."

"Great! Thanks for the information."

"Would you like to make an appointment, Ma'am?"

"Not yet. I'm going to think things over and get back to you."

The recruiter gave me his number and extension so I could make an appointment. I felt as if God had smiled upon me and made it possible for me to have a way out. I had every intention of making this venture work out for us.

It had been about a week since I last saw Mike. I hope I didn't hurt him by rejecting his offer, although this time, it allowed me to think things over.

It was the last week in September when I walked into an Air Force recruiter's office, ready to make the decision that would change my life. He immediately noticed my fortitude and immediately asked if he could help me.

"I want to join the Air Force," I said confidently.

"Great, let's get you started!" he said, shuffling some papers. "Would you mind sitting while I ask you some questions?"

"Sure; how long does it take to get in?" I asked impatiently.

"Are you that anxious?" He smirked.

"I am ready to make a new future for myself and my child."

"I see." He said with a smile.

I filled out mounds of paperwork and reluctantly gave him brief information about my situation.

He suspected I might be overweight, so he weighed me there in the office. He told me we should do what he called a delayed enlistment so I could lose about nine pounds and find a place for my daughter to stay during my training.

My final decision caused some distance between Mike and me.

My mind flooded with what-ifs, and I tried to shove them away long enough to enjoy my remaining time with him.

We spent hours talking about the future and what we both wanted.

"Mike, I need to go, but that doesn't mean you can't meet me wherever I am."

"I have a life here; my family is here. I can't just up and leave."

"But you'll still write?"

"Of course I will. Just because you're leaving doesn't mean I'll fall out of love with you, Betty."

"We'll figure it out. You are the most considerate and understanding man I've ever known, and you love Tracy like she were your own; what more can I ask? I love you so much."

Working together, we found an agency to keep Tracy while I was gone. They suggested foster parents for her and set me up with a list of the available parents in town. I met with three different families and decided on a family without kids. I felt comfortable with them right away. Their home was clean, with a piano in the front room that Tracy could play. The backyard was spacious, and Tracy could play for hours.

They asked me if there were any restrictions on visitations from family or friends. I told them that Mike and Tim could pick Tracy up and spend the day with her. My mother could see her, but she wouldn't be allowed to be alone with her.

Thankfully, they agreed to my conditions without any problems.

The next order of business was payment for their services. I wasn't on welfare, so I didn't get any help with the cost of care. I explained that I got paid every two weeks. They were okay with that, but the amount they charged would take my whole paycheck except twenty dollars. Financially, it would be a struggle, but emotionally, it made me feel better knowing that Tracy has love and kindness: one *challenge down and one to go.*

Over the next few weeks, I starved myself to meet the weight requirement. It drove me crazy, but I stayed away from all the treats.

I also arranged to put all of my belongings into storage. I kept my mattress and box springs to sleep on for two months. Given my financial circumstances, Mom agreed she would pay for my storage.

Fall arrived, and I was getting more nervous as time went on. I knew I had gone too far to turn back now.

Finally, the time came to take the plunge! It was Tracy's fifth birthday party, and my stomach was in knots.

I could tell Mike was having a hard time with it, too. That evening, I had to hand her over to the foster parents. Smiling was excruciating, but I didn't want Tracy's last memory to be of me grimacing on her special day. We had it one day early since I was leaving the next day. Of all the days of the year, her birthday was the only day I could get in.

We pulled up at the foster home, and I took a deep breath, knowing I wouldn't be leaving with my daughter.

I forced my legs to move as I exited the car and held Tracy close. Mike helped with the bags, but I knew he didn't want to leave her either. I brought Tracy here a week ago to get to know the foster parents, and they took to each other right away, but she didn't fully understand why we were coming here this late, so as I put her down, she hovered around me for reassurance.

When it was time for me to leave, Tracy looked terrified as she clutched onto me. I mentioned that I would go on a short trip to get her used to the idea, but she still needed to believe me. I bent down to her, holding her in my arms as I spoke.

"Mommy has to go to work for seven weeks, but I am returning, Honey. Mommy will miss you so much."

I felt the tears streaming down my face, and I knew she sensed something wasn't right. Those big brown eyes did not understand the concept of time. Seven weeks could have been a couple of hours to her, but she still didn't want to be left alone with these people.

"No, Mommy! Don't leave me here." She began to cry.

She clutched even tighter to my neck and letting her go took all my energy.

"Honey, I am not going for a long time, just seven weeks.

Mommy is coming back, I promise.

I am not leaving you forever. Let me do this job, and I will return to you."

"But, Mommy, don't leave me here. I want to go with you."

"Tracy, please, Mommy's coming back for you. Don't be sad."

She wasn't going to understand. I was being ripped apart inside, but I had to keep my eye on the goal.

My choice to leave would be so much better for her down the road. I removed her hands and turned her over to the foster parents. "I love you with all of my heart."

"Mommy, please don't go, Mommy, Mommy!"

My tears blinded me as I turned and walked as fast as possible towards the truck, with Mike following close behind for support. When I got inside, I could still hear her cries for me to return. It was the worst feeling I had ever felt.

Mike squeezed my hand, saying, "She'll be all right; you are doing what you think is right for her."

I was doing this for her.

It was true…I was running away from my past, but I was also running toward our future. I prayed that my baby would forgive me for leaving her with these strangers. Unlike my birth mother, I had no intention of leaving my child for good.

On November 6, 1978, I stepped onto a plane with tear-stained cheeks and bloodshot eyes headed for San Antonio, Texas. One layover and 10 hours later…

"Welcome to San Antonio. The temperature is currently 72 degrees. For those connecting to another flight, find your connecting information inside the terminal. Have a wonderful day, and thank you for flying American Airlines."

I yanked my bag from under my seat and stood up. I started down the aisle. It's still possible to turn back. I could book a return flight and be with Tracy by nightfall. I shifted my bag and prepared to step off the plane. Just then, I felt someone touch my arm.

It was Sandra.

"Everything's gonna be okay, you know."

I smiled at her. Stepping off of the plane, somehow, I knew she was right.

The fork in the road is simple.

One path has deep grooves that you can easily get stuck in. The reward is minimal if there is any. Joyce, Jimmy, Roy, and Debbie took the familiar road.

The other road has obstacles and roadblocks, and you must forge ahead with your tools, but the reward can be immense when the trial is finally over. The road less traveled does not have people full of wisdom waiting to tell you which way to turn. Therefore, at times, you'll get lost and can feel lonely. The short of it is, as human beings, we are worth the effort it takes to become unique and strong individuals. I chose the unmarked path because I had no direction and was unwilling to accept the cards the people in my life expected me to deal with.

As I stepped outside the terminal, I took a deep breath...*This is it.*

"I love you, Tracy," I whispered. "See you in 7 weeks."

THE BEGINNING

Epilogue

Going through all these challenging things has taught me to see tragedy as an opportunity to overcome and triumph. Your struggles become a power to move on, so you learn new ways to knock it down whenever you come to a wall. The walls get smaller and thinner as time passes because you gain confidence with every victory. Eventually, you look at the border and laugh because you know you have what it takes to obliterate it.

On the other hand, if you see a wall, remember that we are born with strength but still have to learn how to overcome it through trial and error. So, the next time you face an inevitable obstacle, remember that this is just another opportunity to help catapult you over the next wall you encounter.

Why try if you believe you can't overcome your situation and it is easier to give up? The problem with this perspective is that if you stay behind the towering problem, the shadow will overwhelm you.

But BEWARE; through conquering these obstacles, I have been guilty of trivializing others' despair. For instance, when we have overcome a situation and see someone else going through the same thing, we want to tell them to "pick yourself up by your bootstraps" and do something about it. We may have found our answers and were strong enough to overcome them, but others may not recognize they have strength. This can cause others to see us as strong-willed, harsh, or not empathetic to their plight.

Remember how you felt so you can keep your heart soft and be careful not to make them feel hopeless by trivializing their situation. Empathize and briefly share your story while giving hope and encouragement to pull them through.

Every day I wake up, I must thank God for another beautiful day and the fact that I would not be here without him. Yes, I went through a lot of chaos in my life, but I can honestly say I would change very few things. I love myself, my children, and all the miraculous things around me.

Aftanoon	afternoon
Ah	Are
Brothas	brothers
Caful	careful
Corna	corner
Ee'as	ears
Etha	either
Floa	floor
Foa	four
Fow	for
Hea	here
Lata	later
Mothas	mothers
Mowa	more
Neva	never
Otha	other
Ova	over
Poc	park
Rememba	remember
Roga	Roger
Septemba	September
Shua	sure
Sistas	sisters
Smalla	smaller
Statted	started
Tha's	there's
Wicka chai	wicker chair
Yawd	yard
Yoa	your
You'a	you are
Waya	Where

www.ingramcontent.com/pod-product-compliance
Lightning Source LLC
Chambersburg PA
CBHW051138120626
46547CB00012B/853